Effective Ministry
as an Associate Pastor

Making
Beautiful Music
as a
Ministry Team

Robert J. Radcliffe

kregel
PUBLICATIONS

Grand Rapids, MI 49501

Effective Ministry as an Associate Pastor: Making Beautiful Music as a Ministry Team

Published by Kregel Publications, a division of Kregel, Inc., P.O. Box 2607, Grand Rapids, MI 49501. Kregel Publications provides trusted, biblical publications for Christian growth and service. Your comments and suggestions are valued.

For more information about Kregel Publications, visit our web site at www.kregel.com.

Cover design: Alan G. Hartman
Book design: Frank Gutbrod

Library of Congress Cataloging-in-Publication Data
Radcliffe, Robert J.
    Effective ministry as an associate pastor: making beautiful music as a ministry team / by Robert J. Radcliffe.
        p.   cm.
    Includes bibliographical references.
    1. Associate clergy.   I. Title.
BV674.R33   1998   253—dc21   98-25984
                                            CIP
ISBN 0-8254-3629-x

Printed in the United States of America

1 2 3 4 / 02 01 00 99 98

Contents

Preface

If you have ever played an instrument in an orchestra, you know what second fiddle means. Both professional and musical training organizations have such a designation. Professional groups are more fixed, but in training organizations, beginning players start at last chair in the lowest part for their instrument and work up. Through successful competitive auditions players move up to the goal of first part and first chair. The competition is fierce.

The first chair for every instrument is the most skilled player for that instrument. It is the person in the first chair who plays the highest part, and the highest part is usually the most difficult. If the instrument is a melody instrument, the first-part players will play it. If the music calls for it, the first-chair player in the first part will perform the solo. First-chair violin is the concert master (or mistress), who has special privileges. First chair, first part is the highest position in that instrument in the whole organization. The person who sits there receives a well-earned respect. Second chair for first part means you are good, but you are not the best. First chair in the second part is not as good as any first-part player. Third-part players are not as good as any second-part player. The pecking order is very clear.

A pastoral staff of a local church is in size closer to an ensemble than an orchestra and is organized much like a musical group. There should be no doubt as to who possesses the first chair or solo part on the pastoral staff—the senior pastor. As in a musical ensemble, various staff members are usually assigned different instruments and therefore play different parts. Each staff member is assigned a different function in the ministry and all are equally important to the overall harmony. Our Lord Jesus Christ could be said to be the composer of the music. When all the instruments are playing the correct part, the music is beautiful and harmonious.

When one part is not being played, there is a gap, an emptiness that is obvious to all. When one instrument plays the music intended for another, the result is a discordant and confusing sound. Depending on the instruments in the ensemble, the group may be experimenting to find their unique sound. It is possible that some pastoral staff members are not even performing the same composition. They may be off somewhere playing their own tune. None of these situations makes for beautiful music.

The comparison of a pastoral staff to a musical ensemble helps us understand the dynamics that occur, but this comparison has some drawbacks. If staff evaluations are auditions for the ensemble, it isn't probable that staff members would request performance evaluations unless they knew they would receive high praise or wished to move to other positions among the same staff. Th] z/»icial board of the church would usually be the conductor of the ensemble. The board would approve any moves by the staff member, but reassignment of staff members to other functions would not likely occur. The lack of specific training or experience would restrict a staff member to one or two tasks. Also, some tasks simply need to be done, so shifting staff members may not be practical. While there may be other weaknesses in this comparison, the idea of beautiful music from a pastoral team that plays in harmony with each other, that complements each other by carrying out various functions, seems to be a model worth exploring.

Associate ministers who occupy the second chair may think that they are something less than a true pastor in a church. They wonder how they can accept a subordinate position and still experience a fulfilling ministry. They wonder if the senior pastor is expected by some to play all the parts in the pastoral ensemble. Isn't there room and even the necessity for some to play the supporting role so that beautiful harmony can emerge from the church staff? And so that two or more are not trying to play the same part and other parts are left unplayed? Can the ministry of the second fiddle be a lifelong calling or is it only appropriate for part of a ministerial career? Associates often struggle over the question of how they will ever make beautiful music as the second fiddle on the church staff. Some may have accepted the myth that beautiful music is just not possible.

It should be no surprise that the associate-pastor role is fraught with great challenges and pitfalls. It is no wonder that many who begin with one instrument (ministry specialty) do not stay with it long enough to master their playing. Lawson's study of 392 associate pastors who filled the role of Christian educators found that of former staff members, 44 percent left the field after one position and another 32 percent left after the second position. The average number of staff positions for this group was 1.86 and the number of years as an associate was 7.16 years. He found that a person left the Christian education associate pastorate at an average age of 36.[1]

Few who take the associate position feel committed to it as a career, that is, in the same ministry speciality. As a person's interests change, so does the ministry. An associate often shifts to another ministry speciality or takes a senior-pastor position. Serving as an associate pastor is more often viewed as a learning experience or stepping stone to the senior pastorate. Various specialities are often viewed as experiments, a sort of trial-and-error approach to ministry. Some who do not have the opportunity to move into the role of senior pastor or solo pastor (also called a single pastor without a paid staff) when they are ready to do so, may become frustrated because they have to settle for the associate role. They will likely feel unfulfilled in their role as associate. After all, they did not aspire to be an associate. The tenure of pastoral-staff members other than the senior pastor is normally much shorter than that of the senior minister in many churches. This may be due to associates continually looking to move chairs or to move to a different ensemble altogether. They may miss the blessing that God has for them right where they are.

Can the associate pastor experience long-term fulfillment and joy as number two, three, or even four? The answer is yes! And in these pages I will disclose exactly how that happens. I will tell you about my personal experiences in the associate pastorate. If you have not guessed by now, I served contentedly in that role for many years as both an unordained associate and as an ordained associate. I am currently a seminary professor involved in full-time training of men and women for the position of associate pastor.

In all my associate-pastor positions, I served as Christian education leader with responsibilities for children, youth, and adult ministries. I also have other pastoral experience such as preaching; church administration, which included budgets, music, evangelism, visitation, counseling, and conducting weddings and funerals; and miscellaneous ministries, such as secretarial and custodial. While my experience is fairly broad as an associate, I recognize that it is still limited to one person's experience. Everything I write here will be filtered through my experience only and can certainly be enriched by the experience of others. I have reviewed the research of others when appropriate and have given them credit when I used their ideas. I am grateful to the many pastors and church leaders who shared with me their experiences. Their input has contributed to the conclusions drawn in the following pages.

Perhaps you are a senior pastor who has worked with associates in the past or are considering calling an associate to work with you for the first time. You also need to gain some insight into the role and challenges of this particular position in the local church. Each chapter should help you better prepare to work with associates in your church, especially if you have never served as an associate yourself.

Perhaps you are currently serving as an associate, and you are a bit frustrated. I have good news for you. You can learn to enjoy your work. You may need to adjust your attitude or understanding, but it is possible to learn how to thrive as an associate. Or you may discover that you're simply not suited for this role and should change your ministry focus. This book is designed to help in that process as well. Be sure to use the discussion questions at the end of each chapter, either by yourself or with others.

Perhaps you are at the beginning of your ministerial career and wondering if God is calling you into an associate pastorate. You may not be sure if you have what it takes. It takes a certain kind of person to be effective and satisfied in this role. You should be able to identify the sort of person who will best succeed in the associate role. Thus, you'll be better equipped to make that decision for yourself. A checklist of questions in Appendix A will help guide you through these issues. The questions in Appendix B will help you determine if it is time for an associate to move on. Appendix C is a list of sequential events that are typical when a church calls an associate pastor.

Whatever your reason for picking up this book, I trust you will be challenged, enlightened, and motivated by considering the beautiful music possible through the ministry of the associate pastor on a local church pastoral staff.

Part 1:
Foundations

CHAPTER ONE

Interpreting the Score
(Biblical/Theological)

In order to play well together, musicians must use the same music or score. Utter confusion and disharmony is the only result when using different musical scores or when trying to play the score written for another instrument. The score places each instrument in the proper key, assuming each is tuned properly, so that they can be played together harmoniously. Beyond that, each player must be on the same page, must play in tempo with others, and must be at the exact same beat of the same measure. The role of each member of the pastoral staff must be taken from the same score or the only thing heard by the congregation is a cacophony. Playing from the same score prevents widespread misunderstanding and misinterpretation for all parties concerned. It could be said that the score we use to define our roles in ministry is the Bible. While this should be, and often is, true, it is a glib and simplistic statement. How the Bible is interpreted to determine specific pastoral roles is the key issue.

Have you ever been asked, "When are you going into the ministry?" I have. The question was disconcerting because I thought I was in ministry at the time. This was in 1964 during my first church position as director of Christian education. Because I had an office located next to the senior pastor's and was serving that local church full time, I thought everyone knew that I was in the ministry. I was a seminary graduate and every day my work involved the spiritual matters of the local church. My total salary was derived from my "ministry," and that money ($100 per week) from the church provided for the support of my wife and myself and later our two small children. I had no other job, and the only other family income was from my wife's part-time job. After our first child arrived, my wife did not work outside the home for a period of twelve years. How could I not be considered to be in the ministry? Maybe it was because I was not ordained.

After four and a half years in my first full-time church, I was asked by the pastor to consider ordination. After I prepared my twenty-page doctrinal statement and was grilled for several hours by local

13

pastors at my ordination council, they voted to approve my ordination by the church that I served. The date was set, and at a special service, I was *ordained* into the ministry by that same church. Now, I thought, *I'll surely be viewed as a full-fledged minister.* I clutched my ordination certificate and left the church within a week after my ordination and moved to a new place of service. The attitudes of some in the new church were communicated to me from the outset. I was definitely not treated as the senior pastor was treated. It was clear he was in the ministry, and I was his assistant. Were people wondering if I was taking the associate position for a short period of time until a "real" or "full" pastorate opened up? Was I second class, somehow not good enough to make it to the first rank, the big time, and be a real, that is, senior pastor. Was that why I had accepted an associate position? If I preferred to serve in a larger church as an associate staff rather than be the solo pastor of a smaller church, was I in a dead-end position?[1] Did this make me someone who had not made it to the pinnacle of my profession? Perhaps I was too young (I was twenty-eight years old) to assume the senior role and needed a little seasoning. These questions about the associate position have many sources, such as bad experiences with previous associates or a comparison with business. Some Christians believe, however, that the associate-ministry role is somehow unbiblical.

Where is the role of associate pastor in Scripture anyway? If it is not mentioned, why do we create such positions in the church? These are important questions, not because people have asked them, but because many times they have *not* been asked. If we assume we should have associates in churches without asking if they are biblically supported, we open the door to creating any pastoral position that we wish. It is not too great a leap to create a minister of anything at all. I would like to show several ways that I think the associate pastor role has support from a biblical and theological point of view.

Multiple Elders

The title of pastor in our churches has evolved from the New Testament. The term *elder* comes from the Greek word *presbuteros*. The term can have different meanings, and one is used adjectivally to denote seniority as in Luke 15:25 and 1 Timothy 5:2. Elder also refers to that group of Jewish men, usually associated with scribes and Pharisees, who were responsible for the synagogue (Matt. 16:21; 27:12). The final meaning refers to a group of men who were appointed to hold an office in the early church for the purpose of exercising spiritual oversight (Acts 14:23; 20:17). The term *elder* seems to be used interchangeably with the term for bishop, with elder referring to the person and bishop (or overseer) emphasizing what the elder does.[2]

Clyde E. Harrison states that "before the first century A.D. had elapsed, the term 'bishop' had taken on a special meaning, denoting the one leader of a church. This situation is illustrated both in the book of Acts and in Paul's epistles in the person of James, the brother of Jesus, who was obviously the head man in the Jerusalem Church."[3] If this is true, then very early in the church, the idea of multiple elders had vanished, if it had ever existed. I believe there is sufficient biblical evidence that multiple elders did serve the early church, especially assisting in the ministry of Paul.

One of the first names that comes to mind as an associate in Paul's ministry is Timothy, his son in the faith. Paul and Timothy traveled and ministered together; both are mentioned in the letter to the Philippians (1:1). Another individual, Silvanus, was Paul's coworker when the two letters to Thessalonica were written (1 Thess. 1:1 and 2 Thess. 1:1). Barnabas was appointed to travel with Paul on the first missionary journey (Acts 13:2, 13), and later Paul joined with Silas to continue the work (Acts 15:40). After John Mark was not allowed to go with Paul, the former linked up with Barnabas, and Paul went with Silas. Some of Paul's associates also included Priscilla and Aquila (Acts 18:18) and Apollos (Acts 19:1). The Ephesian elders might be considered associates or coworkers with Paul, having served with him for several years (Acts 20:17–18). Euodia and Syntyche must have been coworkers with Paul (Phil. 4:2) as was Clement (Phil. 4:3). Paul had many associates, and many, if not all, could be considered part of a multiple-elder team that served in various places.

The reference in Philippians 4:3 to "my true comrade" (NASB) or "loyal yokefellow" (NIV) is from the Greek word *suzugos*, which the Analytical Greek Lexicon translates "associate" or "fellow-laborer."[4] Arndt and Gingrich, however, give more options for the meaning of this word.[5] The first use of the term is a proper name. Eugene Peterson's *The Message*, a modern English translation, follows this meaning. Arndt and Gingrich said Clement of Alexandria and Origen thought this name was a specific person, Paul's wife. A second meaning from Arndt and Gingrich is for the opponent of a gladiator and follows the Latin, *commilito*. Arndt and Gingrich supply a third meaning, quoting Lohmeyer, who thought the word meant a brother in suffering since Paul was in prison. In examining the various usages, Arndt and Gingrich claim there is much support for the proper-name view.[6] Even if the proper-name view is used for the meaning of *suzugos*, the fact that Paul was referring to a fellow worker or associate cannot be denied. In fact, any of the options supplied by Arndt and

Gingrich can be viewed as a type of associate whom Paul had in his ministry.

Another source for the idea of multiple elders in the early church grew out of the Greek title *episkopos*, often translated bishop. Lightfoot declared that "in Athenian language it was used especially to designate commissioners appointed to regulate a new colony or acquisition."[7] Arndt and Gingrich say that another word for bishop might be *guardian* or *superintendent*.[8] When considering the word elder, Lightfoot explains:

> In the lifetime of the law giver, in the days of the judges, throughout the monarchy, during the captivity, after the return, and under Roman domination, the "elders" appear as an integral part of the governing body of the country. . . . Over every Jewish synagogue . . . a council of "elders" presided. It was not unnatural, therefore, when the Christian synagogue took its place by the side of the Jewish, a similar organization should be adopted with such modifications as circumstances required; and thus the name familiar in the old dispensation was retained under the new.[9]

After the pioneering work of the apostle, prophet, evangelist, and pastor-teacher[10] were well under way in the church at large, elders were appointed in every local church (see Acts 14:23). The instruction in 1 Peter 5:1–3 refers to the functions and character of the elder serving as pastor, but does not limit the function to one person in each congregation. In fact, the passage begins by addressing a plurality of elders. This could, of course, be referring to all of the elders of individual churches as recipients of a general letter without implying there was more than one elder per congregation. Is there more clear support for multiple elders and thus for associate pastors in one congregation? Barnabas and Saul (Paul) were itinerants but also pastored by teaching for extended periods in one church. They taught for one year in Antioch (Acts 11:26). It appears that the pastoral role included a team of at least two teaching elders. Which pastor-elder did what, and who was the senior and who was the associate is unclear. Barnabas was named first at the outset and later Saul (who became Paul) was mentioned first. Perhaps they reversed ministry roles. Who performed which role is irrelevant; the point is that they both served as pastors in the same church.

Those who question having more than one pastor per congregation fail to recognize that since the inception of the church there were multiple elders who functioned together as equals. The elders at Ephesus were equals before the Lord; any difference was in functions. Consider Paul, who traveled with various persons on his missionary journeys. They served as equals before the Lord but differed in their functions. Getz firmly declares "that we always see a plurality of leadership" in the New Testament church. There is no reference to the appointment of "one" elder or "one" deacon for any given church.[11] That leaves the question: Which role comprises the associate-pastor role? The answer lies in several other issues.

Elder Roles

The list of gifted persons given in Ephesians 4:11–13 includes apostle, prophet, evangelist, and pastor-teacher. Are these gifted persons active in the church today? Getz posits that these gifted persons such as existed in the early church are not active in the church today. They possessed "greater gifts" and were crucial to the foundation of the early church. For example, Getz makes much of the roles of gifted men, such as the prophet. An elder in today's church does not, according to Getz, receive supernatural inspiration to communicate God's truth, particularly as it relates to future events, as did the prophet.[12] The special gifts of prophecy mentioned in 1 Corinthians 12 and Ephesians 4 refer to a special group of individuals in New Testament days. Like the gift of apostleship, prophecy was a "foundational" gift.[13]

While Getz claims that the elders of the early church were never classified as having these greater gifts, nevertheless they were in many respects to do the same type of work as an apostle, prophet, evangelist, and pastor-teacher. Like apostles, they were to exhort and defend the faith. The elders were to perform a prophetic ministry, speaking for the truth of the Word of God. They were to proclaim Jesus Christ to the unsaved world, both by life and by verbal witness. They were to teach the Word of God and shepherd the flock in each local congregation.[14]

If the above model is considered, it appears that each of the roles of the elder is indeed present in the church of today, at least in modified form. The elders who serve in the apostolic role will function using some other definitions of that word, such as a messenger, ambassador, or delegate.[15] The modern equivalent might be called, among other things, a missionary or church planter, extending the gospel where it has not been before.

The role of the prophet could be interpreted as the one who announces the Good News as those did who were dispersed by persecution (Acts 11:20). Another way for the modern prophet to function in the church today is to be a forth-teller rather than a foreteller who predicts future events. The prophet as forth-teller is a role the modern pastor can fulfill as he preaches the truth of the Word of God, tailored to the needs of his congregation.

Another elder role that can be utilized in the local church today is that of evangelist. Telling others of the good news of the gospel is a task needed today as much as it was in the first century. Doesn't every elder desire to do the work of an evangelist and have the privilege of leading others to a saving knowledge of Jesus Christ? The Good News becomes even better when it is seen against the evil of our present time. Evangelism certainly can be an elder role practiced in the church today.

The pastor-teacher role has excellent support throughout both Testaments, and the pastor-teacher is a biblical figure with a rich heritage. The first half of the role is pastor. Peter encourages the elders in his first letter to "be shepherds of God's flock that is under your care, serving as overseers—not because you must, but because you are willing, as God wants you to be; not greedy for money, but eager to serve; not lording it over those entrusted to you, but being examples to the flock" (1 Peter 5:2–3).

The shepherd is not a cattle driver but a kinder and gentler leader of sheep. Servanthood is strongly implied in describing the pastor as a shepherd. Peter was told by Jesus to "feed my lambs," "take care of my sheep," and "feed my sheep" (John 21:15–17). The allusion to shepherds and the flock imply, among other things, a ministry of caring and compassion. Caring for the flock of God is certainly a part of the pastor's ministry.

The other half of the role is teacher. The church of today needs the solid teaching of biblical truth. In a day of bizarre and curious cultic beliefs, the church needs God's truth more than ever. Helping others teach well multiplies the teaching ministry. The training and administrative elements of a well-designed teaching ministry is vitally important to helping the church remain strong and true to the Word of God. The elder role of teacher, therefore, is a vital need in the church today.

Any of these roles can, of course, be present in a person's life singly or in various combinations. For example, the role of pastor-teacher does not exclude a use of church planting, evangelistic, or prophetic roles, but separate individuals could certainly focus on any of the roles. Depending on the size of the congregation and the number of elders in a congregation, any of the roles could be assigned to various elders who specialize in that particular type of ministry. In very large congregations, it is not inconceivable that more than one elder would be ministering in each of these roles. Why can't an associate pastor fill any one of these roles? It seems obvious that they certainly can if they are qualified. Let's look at some types of qualifications.

Spiritual Giftedness

Every believer in Jesus Christ has been given a spiritual gift. Romans 12:6 states that "since we have gifts that differ according to the grace given to us, let each exercise them accordingly . . ." (NASB). In this same passage about the body of Christ, Paul speaks of the role of spiritual giftedness. The presence of a gifted person who carries out a role in the church does not exclude others from using their gifts in another role in the same church. In fact, the health of the whole body of Christ depends on believers functioning harmoniously together.

It is clear from Scripture that the purpose of spiritual gifts is to enrich and edify the church (1 Cor. 12:7), and the implication is that no one today has all the gifts. It also seems obvious that there is more than one way to enrich and edify the church. Many pastors will agree that there are certain functions required of them for which they are not as spiritually gifted as others are. Why not look for associates who are spiritually gifted to carry out the functions for which the senior pastor is not gifted? This will free both the senior and associate to function according to their gifts. This should result in more being done and in a sweet harmony from their ministries.

The instruction to gifted persons to equip (train, prepare) the saints for the work of ministry does not require that church members become a cheering section for those who are paid staff. Every believer is to be equipped to do the work of ministry. Depending on his or her gifts, every believer is "on staff"—a member of God's orchestra. The paid staff is responsible for preparing the believers to be as effective in their service to God as is possible. A wide variety of persons within the local church are needed to help believers serve the Lord with their various gifts.

The associate can be vital to the leadership of the church even without being the gifted person who is the "mouthpiece" (forth-teller) for Christ. The concept of the body of Christ in Scripture requires the church to value the less-apparent parts of the body as much as some of the more visible or public parts. Paul said that each person cannot be expected to fulfill every function of the body. Does the hand function as a foot or an ear as an eye? Is there not enough work in the kingdom of God for the many functions of the body? Multiple functions are implied in the imagery of the body of Christ. This seems to be the clear teaching of 1 Corinthians 12:12 and following.

Making Disciples

Jesus commanded us to make disciples (Matt. 28:19–20), and to do this, believers must go beyond leading someone to Christ. Jesus demonstrated by his own ministry that his followers are to help new believers grow up into spiritual maturity so that there will be another generation of believers. In fact, without succeeding generations of believers, the church would have shriveled and died after the first generation was gone.

It should be clear that one person cannot train everyone effectively in a larger church. There is often a need for associates to focus on certain groups, such as youth, children, men, women, singles, or families or to focus on a specific aspect of ministry, such as evangelism, worship, or education. There is a need for associates to focus on helping all believers grow in their faith and take their positions as spiritual leaders within the body of Christ. There is plenty of work for an associate to do in preparing the body of Christ for its ministry. Associates can multiply ministry among the body of Christ by reaching those who might be overlooked. The command to make disciples implies a need for associates.

Character Qualities

Another qualification for elder is quality of character. Elders should be selected for their character, not some role that they have been hired to fulfill. First Timothy 3:1–7 and Titus 1:7–9 list twenty-two qualities of character that an elder must possess (see chap. 3). These qualities are not spiritual gifts, elements of a job description, or an expression of a self-determined call to ministry. There is no reference in either of these passages to education, social standing, or financial situation as a prerequisite for being an elder (which is equivalent to bishop or pastor). To desire the office of pastor is a "good thing," but simply desiring it does not make one qualified. The fully qualified associate must meet all of these qualifications of Scripture to serve as a pastor.

One quality that is pertinent to the associate pastor is that he or she not be a recent convert (1 Tim. 3:6). The age of the associate is often a factor in determining suitability for the senior-pastor position. If a person is too young to be a senior pastor with responsibilities over a staff, then is that person old enough to be a solo pastor (single pastor with no staff)? If he or she is deemed too young to be a solo pastor, the associate position can provide the experience needed. No matter how old a person is in the Lord, someone only in their twenties may be viewed as too young to be an elder. The associate role, therefore, is often viewed as a good starting point for the young leader.

Other qualities of character mentioned by Paul are important for the pastor, but being the "husband of one wife" implies some additional considerations. If the view of Gene Getz is followed regarding this quality, the pastor will be a "one-woman" man. Getz interprets this to mean that the elder should be faithful to one woman.[16] This raises some questions for the associate.

Some say that since an unmarried man cannot be a one-woman man, he is excluded from being a pastor. I believe what Paul meant is that if a man is married, he is to be faithful to his wife all his life. If marriage was a prerequisite to serve in the ministry, Paul himself would not qualify because it cannot be confirmed that he was married. It is not required that an associate be married in order to qualify to be an elder or associate. There are many who exhibit the character qualities of an elder and are not one-woman men because they have chosen celibacy. While some churches may wish that a candidate for associate pastor become married, there is no biblical support for requiring it. A single associate is certainly an option for a church to consider.[17]

Another question raised by the one-woman man requirement of elders is that of divorce. Being faithful to one woman implies that the divorced elder is disqualified for service as an associate pastor. But if the elder or associate becomes divorced while in ministry, are there not situations where faithfulness to one woman may still be maintained? For example, if the woman left the elder or associate and he sought reconciliation throughout, he could retain his devotion and love for her and be faithful to her even though she abandoned him. Divorce while in ministry, per se, might not disqualify him from service. Unfaithfulness to his wife should.

What about an elder-associate who is divorced before becoming a Christian or before becoming a candidate for a church position? Churches often dismiss such candidates without looking into the situation. Again, it is the faithfulness of the elder toward his wife that is the issue. For example, if the elder or associate candidate has not remarried and maintains his love and devotion to his wife, he is a one-woman man. If the wife abandoned the husband, then the elder or associate is still a one-woman man, even if living apart from his wife. Before rejecting a candidate out of hand, churches should look beyond the surface to determine if he fulfills the requirement of being a one-woman man.[18]

Conclusion

There are several biblical and theological arguments for having associate pastors in a local church: the existence of multiple elders in a single church, the roles of elders in a local congregation, spiritual giftedness God distributes to all believers in the body of Christ, the need for disciples rather than converts, and the qualities of character that are necessary for elders in a local church.

All of these biblical and theological views (and others not mentioned) are filtered through various church traditions so that church leadership varies widely in style and kind of organization. In fact, the next chapter deals with some of these variations as they apply to how others have played the part of associate pastor in various church traditions.

Discussion Questions

Use these questions privately or in a group, such as a church staff, to apply the points made in this chapter.

1. Think about your church pastoral staff and describe (orally or in writing) what the duties of each person actually are. Describe what each does on a week-to-week basis, rather than what they are supposed to do. If you do not know what these duties are, find out. If you have no list of duties, write such a list for your situation.

2. Now compare your answer to question one to the elder roles of apostle, prophet, evangelist, pastor, or pastor-teacher. How do the actual duties for each staff member compare to the elder roles, and how are they different?

3. What would you say are the basic reasons for the similarity or dissimilarity between your answers to questions one and two?

4. Do you believe the associate pastor should be an elder or be viewed as one? Give your reasons.

5. What spiritual gifts are best suited for the role of associate pastor and why?

6. How does the need for making reproducing disciples rather than converts support the importance of the associate pastor?

7. Why should associate pastors meet the same level of character qualities that are expected of senior pastors?

8. Which of the reasons for the existence of an associate pastor in a local church has the most validity for you and your ministry? List the reasons for your choice.

9. What other biblical or theological reasons can you think of that support the ministry of an associate pastor in a local church?

CHAPTER TWO

How Have Others
Played This Part?
(Church Traditions)

If everyone understood the role of associate pastors in the same way, think of the unanimity there would be. Soaring cadences of beautiful sounds would fill the air. Besides the Bible, however, there is another foundational source of understanding for the role of the associate pastor. This important area is found in the traditions of individual churches or groups of churches. If a church is a part of a denomination, there are traditions that each church shares with the others. Even nonaffiliated churches develop these types of traditions, albeit independently.

It is amazing how rapidly new churches develop traditions that govern how they function. One may ask, If we have always done our business in a certain way, what is wrong with that? Others may be misled, but how can *our* traditions be wrong? Where church traditions are concerned, how has the church typically viewed the role of the associate? Regardless of denomination, most churches have general principles of church tradition that govern how the associate part is played.[1]

Church Polity

Various types of church polity have defined the role of the associate pastor. The first type is congregational polity, which usually would be Congregational, Baptist, and Independent churches. This type gives the most responsibility to the church as a whole in the calling and supervision of the associate pastor. This polity invites the whole congregation to participate in the call of the associate. The implication is that the congregation will share in the responsibility for the oversight of the associate's ministry; thus each member of the congregation might think he or she has some say about how the associate goes about his or her work. Some members of the congregation might think that they are a kind of employer and the associate is the employee. The congregational form of polity has been the most frequent style used by churches to call and supervise associate pastors.

24

Another type of church polity is the representative or elder-run church, usually associated with the historic Presbyterian model. The representative polity separates the associate from the people one more level than the congregational polity in that the people have less of a direct role in the call and supervision of the associate. In the representative polity, the elders function as the employers and the associate as the employee. The associate reports to the elder board and senior pastor and not directly to the church body. The congregation under this policy would probably tell the elders if they had a concern about the supervision of the associate.

A third type of church polity follows a hierarchical or episcopal system and usually is associated with Anglican, Episcopal, or Methodist churches. The episcopal polity has a bishop or superintendent who appoints pastoral leaders into specific churches. In some church fellowships, this is often done at a certain time of the year. The associate in this type of polity will have a different kind of relationship with the church. The associate could be seen in the hierarchical system as a "junior member" of the fraternity of ministers. It is the bishop (or equivalent) who assigns pastors to churches and often the associates as well. Lines of authority for the associate may be stronger with the person who makes the appointment than with the congregation that is served. Of the three, the episcopal polity places the congregation in the weakest position in regard to the call and supervision of the associate. The senior pastor and the official church board may be the supervisor of the associate, but in case of trouble, the bishop or superintendent will be consulted for advice.

There are numerous variations of these three main types, but the associate must be aware of the type of church polity that is doing the calling. The polity of the church will normally dictate how the associate is supervised and how any disputes or conflicts are resolved. For example, there are many churches that have had a long history of congregational rule and have recently attempted to shift to elder rule. The deacons become elders and the church constitution is updated to reflect the changes of elder rule. The majority of the congregation may have even voted to approve the changes. These changes may simply be cosmetic, however, if the congregation still believes that they should be consulted for major decisions, such as the calling of a pastoral-staff member. If the congregation is simply introduced to the new associate without widespread congregational support for the call, the associate may not be aware of the lack of support for the assigned ministry. It is crucial to know what kind of actual church polity is at work when the associate is called. It could make a world of difference in the effectiveness of the associate.

Most of the churches that called me to serve as an associate were congregational in polity, but two were not. My first ministry position (part-time) was with an elder-run church, but I never met with them nor was I interviewed by them. The entire process was handled by the senior pastor. In the other elder-run church, the elder board interviewed me after the senior pastor had met with me several times. In both cases, my coming to the church was not voted on by the congregation. I was simply introduced to the congregation as the new associate. They were informed when I began and told in general what I would do, but they had little to do with deciding if I would be appointed. It was an accomplished fact.

The congregational polity of the other churches I served handled the filling of the associate position very differently. The senior pastor usually made the first contact and the search committee followed up. When it was determined that I was the one they were going to recommend, a church-wide visit was arranged. I was asked to speak to, meet with, and be interviewed by a broad array of the constituencies of the church. There were meetings with the Christian education committee, the Sunday school teachers, the deacons, the youth groups, the women's groups, the men's groups, and often a general group for any not included in the special meetings.

The difference between these two polities affected my work as an associate in these churches and extended beyond the initial interview and the commencement of the work. I believe the congregational polity required the involvement of a larger number of the church members in understanding the details of my ministry description, in knowing me and my family as individuals, and in making a bigger commitment to the general support of my specific ministry in the church.

The Business Hierarchy

Another foundational influence that is important for understanding the place of an associate pastor in a church may originate outside the church, in government and the business world. Business and government have provided a model for leaders and employees in America that generally follows a hierarchical structure. This model may have created a faulty perception of clerical authority.

Most people in the United States are familiar with the way businesses are typically structured. In a large corporation of long history, the board of directors hires a president or chief executive officer (CEO). This person reports to, and carries out the directives of, the board and usually hires others to serve as subordinates. The subordinates (usually vice presidents) are given a segment of corporate responsibility such as finance, personnel, manufacturing, purchasing, customer service, and so forth. Vice presidents in turn hire staff to carry out the responsibilities given to them. People are hired down the line to the lowliest employee in the corporation. Salaries usually match the differing levels of responsibility. Most Americans are familiar with business hierarchies as well as those of state and federal government, so it is easy to think of the church in a similar way.

If church leaders are not scrupulously careful, they may begin thinking of themselves as a board of directors, the chairman of the board as their president, and the pastor as their chief executive officer. Most, if not all, church leaders will be very familiar with corporate structures from their own experiences. The associate is easily identified with the role of vice president (VP) or perhaps chief operating officer (COO). No associate is ever confused with the CEO.

The idea of an associate's serving in a VP role and having equal standing with the senior pastor who serves as CEO is absurd. The VP is not the equal of the CEO in rank, responsibility, salary, or benefits. Other associate pastors may be added to the church staff as VPs when more direct control is needed over a growing church program, but as long as any associate is perceived as a VP in the organization, equality is likewise preposterous.

One church I served had two boards, one of overseers (elders) and another called deacons. The division of labor was clear. The overseers functioned as a board of directors would in a corporation, supervising the work of the staff, the buildings and grounds, and the finances of the church. The deacons were responsible for the spiritual oversight of the congregation, each being responsible for a portion of the whole church body. This division of function created an unfortunate separation between the spiritual work of the church leaders from the mundane. The two boards did not meet together, so any decisions about new associates was handled by the overseers, and the deacons were not consulted. The overseers wielded far more decision-making power in that church than did the deacons.

Associate pastors may envision themselves as a kind of independent contractor and as an equal with everyone on the church staff. In most polities, however, few on the official board or in the congregation will perceive any associate as the equal of the senior pastor. Associates are often thought of as functionaries of the ecclesiastical organization operated by the specific polity of the church. The congregational polity may create a taskmaster out of every member of the church with the associate feeling like an employee. The representative polity would very likely perceive the associate as an employee of the elder board. The associate appointed by the bishop or superintendent is apt to be more loyal to the association of ministers than to the local church. The polity of the church will dictate the way in which the associate is called, how the task is assigned, how it is understood by the congregation, and how the associate is supervised.

The Holy Man

Another foundational source of understanding (or misunderstanding) for the position of the associate comes from the tradition of "the cleric" in our society. The Protestant "man of the cloth" derived his distinctive role as a successor of the Roman Catholic priest. The idea of a man dedicated to God as somehow more "holy" than the rest of us still lies behind the idea of the modern Protestant clergy. The Roman Catholic vows of poverty, chastity, and obedience are not officially enforced in Protestant churches, but similar expectations for the church staff are present nevertheless.

While ministers are not as highly esteemed by the world as they once were, ministers are still looked up to by the majority of their congregants. The highest esteem that Protestant church members possess for their ordained ministers usually goes to the senior pastor. This is not because the associate may not be qualified to deserve it, but rather because it is not the normal and traditional procedure. In short, giving the associate the highest esteem does not, in the minds of the majority of church members, match the concept of church leadership. If they accept the belief that the senior pastor is somehow more holy than the rest of the congregation, how can there be more than one holy man in each congregation? Larger churches were at one time smaller ones and small churches only have one holy man. It is difficult for people to shift their thinking just because the church has grown in size. The cleric in the past may have worn special vestments to distinguish him from the laity. He would also have been the only one allowed to officiate at sacerdotal functions and mount the sacred stairs to speak from the high, sacred pulpit.

Even in churches where vestments and a divided chancel have been replaced with casual clothes and a single, central pulpit or a clear plastic one (or no pulpit furniture at all) on a low stage, it is the speaker at the majority of worship services who is thought of as the senior pastor no matter what the title may be. Others on the church staff who do not speak from the authority of the Bible before the congregation on a regular basis cannot fill the senior-pastor role of forth-telling that the regular pastor does. Even if the associate pastor occasionally fills the pulpit, the people usually assume there is only one pastor, the senior pastor.

Confusion over pastoral roles becomes noticeable when there are two who serve as copastors on the same staff. Even if preaching responsibilities are equally divided, the congregation begins to segregate along lines of preference. Some may say, "I like pastor so and so because he is so down-to-earth." Others may disagree and prefer the other preacher because he "gives us the meat of the Word." Church splits have occurred over preferences for one copastor over another because the view persists that church leadership is a hierarchy and that there is only one holy man per church. If duties on the pastoral staff were more traditionally divided with one doing all the preaching, there would be less cause for comparison and less reason for division. Associates may feel, however, that they are not full players in the ensemble. In one church constitution I have read, the senior pastor is given full control to hire staff "to assist him in his duties." The staff personnel are called assistants rather than associates, and the ministry description of each assistant is entirely left up to the senior pastor to determine. When an assistant is called, the deacons of this church approve the recommendation of the senior pastor, and the church votes to affirm the recommendation of the deacons.

It appears that in this church of congregational polity the hierarchical model of the pastor as chief executive officer is combined with that of the holy man. Consider what would happen if the senior pastor's recommendation is rejected by the deacons or the congregation. The senior pastor would likely question his ability to lead this congregation. The approval of a new assistant or the reassignment of duties of a current assistant could be an important litmus test for congregational support of the senior pastor. The arrangement required by this church constitution assumes that there is only one pastor per congregation and that the senior pastor intuitively knows who should be called as his assistants and what each will do. The deacons have veto power, but likely would not use it unless there was a power struggle. The congregation normally rubber-stamps the deacons' recommendation, but that is not always a foregone conclusion. When beloved assistants have their ministry descriptions shuffled or are asked to resign, majority approval by the congregation may not be forthcoming.

The title that is used by most associates who are ordained is "pastor" (at least this was my experience). If the senior pastor believes there is one holy man in the congregation, the associate might be referred to publicly as brother or sister so and so, or by his or her first name. The congregation will usually follow the lead of the senior pastor in referring to the associate. The name used for the associate by the senior pastor and church board usually indicates whether status of holy man (or woman) is afforded the associate.

The holy-man syndrome is another factor the associate must evaluate in the call to a new church. The associate must take into consideration the holy-man syndrome when the issues of supervision and evaluation are considered.

History of Predecessors

Another element in the tradition of the church is the history of predecessors. If the associate is considering a position with no predecessor, the associate is carving out new territory within that church. The first associate position in a church is experimental, and the first associate might, therefore, become a sacrificial lamb. There will be no predecessor to compare the associate with, either favorably or unfavorably. Comparison will be made, of course, to the senior pastor or to associates from other churches, but there will be no one who has served in that church as an associate who will constitute a bench mark.

The church that has had no former associate is usually smaller, but growing, which is the major reason the associate is called. The hope is that the calling of an associate will bring more growth to the church; thus the financial cost of the associate will more easily be covered. The senior pastor may or may not have had previous experience with an associate. If he has, the associate will be measured against the senior pastor's former associates. If the senior pastor has had no previous experience with an associate, there may be mythical or ideal expectations for the new associate.

The church that has had former associates presents another type of church tradition. If the church is rich with history, the list of associates might be long. Descriptions of the associates' duties may have varied over the years, and the number of associates on the church staff would have risen and fallen parallel to the size of the church. A church with a tradition of a certain number of associates with certain assigned duties may find it difficult to change either. Is the associate being asked to fill a newly created position in a historic church? Is the associate being asked to fill a position that many others have filled in the past? Is the church trying to hang on to tradition by seeking to fill an associate position that is not needed anymore? What has been the tenure of the previous associates? Why did they leave the position?

These are significant questions, because the history of predecessors in the associate role can provide important insights about church tradition that will be valuable to the associate. The questions may be directed to the senior pastor, search committee, the official church board, or to general church members. The best source of information would be the associate who was the immediate predecessor. These persons will usually have no reason to withhold information regarding the position they have vacated. If the position title, duties, or amount of time required to do the job have been changed, the predecessor can discuss the reasons. Any issue related to the traditions of the church that is seeking to fill an associate position could also be discussed with a predecessor.

In my first full-time church-staff position, my predecessor had been killed in a terrible auto accident. It was a year before the church could begin to think about replacing him. I could not interview my predecessor in this situation, and it was difficult for the people in the church to talk about his ministry. When I first arrived, much of the predecessor's books and files were still in the office. I was able to construct the ministry of this person as I examined his files. As time passed, I learned more about his style of ministry from members of the church. It was strange to be discovering the ministry of a man I had never known.

It also became clear to me that I was being compared to my predecessor. In fact, I learned, after I left the church, that I was selected because it was thought by some that I could bring to those areas of ministry some abilities that were lacking in my predecessor. Some thought he was too desk-bound and needed to be more hands-on. I was a bit surprised to be told years later that I had been utilized to accomplish an agenda totally unknown to me. I did not feel manipulated, but the fact that my predecessor in this church had died preempted any attempt on my part to understand how our two ministries would correspond. I had to rely on other ways to discover how my job description compared to that of my predecessor.

Women as Associates

Another element of denominational or local church tradition is whether the associate is a man or a woman. Those groups of churches that from the beginning of their existence have had women in their leadership as senior pastors do not struggle with women as associates. The Foursquare denomination was founded by a woman, Aimee Semple McPherson. While she functioned as an evangelist, she also was the senior pastor of a large church in Los Angeles for many years. The wives of male senior pastors in that denomination and in other churches (such as the Assemblies of God) also are often viewed as equal pastors or associates to their husbands. But what about a woman associate who is not married to the pastor or perhaps is not married at all?

Women as associate pastors are becoming increasingly common in more denominations as well as in churches not aligning themselves with a denomination. Women not related to any of the pastors and who serve on a church staff are usually limited to children's work, or in some cases, youth, small groups, women's ministry, or general Christian education ministry. There are few female general associates in evangelical churches (with the exceptions mentioned above and others) who are ordained because of the sacerdotal functions that the woman would then be expected to fulfill. Women often serve in a limited area of responsibility in the United States even if they are spiritually, and in every other way, qualified to serve in a greater capacity. It is interesting that women who serve as foreign missionaries often have greater pastoral responsibilities overseas than they are allowed in the United States.

Women serving as associate pastors are thought to be limited by scriptural injunctions, the chief of which is 1 Timothy 2:9–15. Schreiner offers the explanation that this passage is clear that women should learn silently and submissively and forbids women to teach or exercise authority over men.[2] This author does make a distinction between a woman's being called to the ministry and being called to be a pastor.[3] According to this view, the former is acceptable and the latter not. If the woman is not ordained as a pastor and no sacerdotal function is expected or required, the sex of the associate is not an issue. Only when ordination and the expected accompanying sacerdotal functions are present in the situation does sex make a difference.

I believe the ordination of women is a local church decision and should be decided using each church's own criteria. A basic factor influencing the decision is the interpretation of biblical passages such as 1 Timothy 2:9–15, 1 Timothy 3:1–7, and Titus 1:7–9.[4] Each church tradition also factors into the decision-making process. Other issues too numerous to mention here also affect the outcome of the local church decision, but the decision remains that of the local church.

Even when the traditional view is followed, as in the book *Women in the Church*, the door remains open for women to serve as associates.

> The church has generally agreed that 1 Timothy 2:11–15 at least prohibits women from functioning as teaching and ruling pastors or elders, but even among those who espouse the historic view, there have been differences regarding the application of this text to other circumstances.[5]

These other circumstances should include women who serve on a church staff in a role other than that of a teaching or ruling pastor or elder. Men serve as associates in nonteaching or nonruling pastor roles and women should not be excluded from them merely because of their sex. Women can and should be called to (and serve in) ministry in the local church without being a senior pastor.

Another scriptural barrier to a woman's serving as associate pastor is the one that requires being married to "one wife." If single men are allowed to be pastors, then the qualification of being married to one wife should not eliminate single women either. Is the inability of a woman to be a "one-woman man" the usual reason women are excluded from the associate role? No, they are often excluded by the same traditions and perspectives that limit their male counterparts. A married woman in the role of associate pastor can be measured against the same standard—that she is a one-man woman.

If the associate is not required or allowed to exercise sacerdotal functions, then it matters little if the associate is male or female, single or married. If the function of the associate is clearly circumscribed and sacerdotal functions are not included in the ministry description, women often find positions as associate staff members, but perhaps not general associate pastors. Many women can be found in church staff positions where those positional roles are clearly prescribed, such as children's director, youth director, director of Christian education, visitation, music, counseling, or women's ministries. These roles can be either unordained positions or licensed positions. Any of these positions can be part-time or full-time.

It is true that women in ministry suffer more severe limitations and restrictions on their ministry (such as fewer responsibilities and less salary or benefits), but both sexes suffer restrictions due to the perception of the role of associate pastors. We need to ask: Is the issue that a candidate for the associate position is female or is it that the position requires sacerdotal functions? It seems that if a church is willing to limit the role of the associate to nonsacerdotal functions (usually the director level), there should be no problem with the selection due to sex. If the church tradition excludes women from ordination and/or from serving as senior pastors, it does not seem necessary to exclude women from all forms of ministry that are performed by associates.

Conclusion

So it can be said that there are significant issues from church tradition that affect having an associate pastor in a local church. There are a wide variety of church polities, the acceptance in our society of the business hierarchy, the tradition of one cleric in the church, the history of predecessors, and women as associates. Church traditions are an important part of how the associate pastor can play beautiful music.

Discussion Questions

Use these questions privately or in a group, such as a church staff, to apply the points made in this chapter.

1. What type of church polity is actually at work in your church as it relates to the call of the associate? How can you tell?

2. Is your pastoral staff viewed by the church board as equals with different functions or as employees of the religious corporation?

3. Is the view of the congregation supported by the church constitution or does tradition of the church contradict the constitution?

4. What effect does the view of the congregation have on staff-member effectiveness and fulfillment, particularly that of the associate's?

5. Does your church presume that there is only one holy man on your church staff? Is the senior pastor perceived by the congregation as qualitatively different than the other members of the church staff?

6. What effect does the general view of the church about the holy man have on the functioning of the staff? What evidence can you cite to support your answers to these questions?

7. Are there members of your church staff who do not fully contribute to the beautiful music that should be coming from the pastoral staff? Would a change of their functions or roles benefit the church or the associate?

8. Is your church run as a business with a CEO or COO for a senior pastor or more like a musical ensemble where everyone has a specific part to play for the benefit of the whole?

9. What can you conclude about the associate's position in your church from the history of predecessors?

10. What is your attitude about having women in the ministry of associate pastor?

CHAPTER THREE

What Is the Condition of My Instrument?
(The Minister)

E very musician in the orchestra should demonstrate a concern for the condition of his or her own instrument. Professional musicians, those who make their living from performing, usually want to purchase the finest instrument they can afford. Violinists want the best, such as a Stradivarius. Once obtained, the instrument receives meticulous attention: it is cleaned, polished, repaired immediately when broken, and transported as safely as possible. Musicians want their instruments to be perfect as long as possible. When the musician finds that the instrument cannot sound the finest tone or perform to the highest standards demanded by the musician, he or she will try to find a better one.

Character

I would like to suggest that the instrument of the associate pastor is himself or herself, specifically the character and personality of the individual. It is the associate's inner self that dictates how well the associate will perform. The associate must keep his or her character in top form to perform at peak efficiency for the glory of God. Associates cannot get another instrument but can repair or improve the ones they have. The instrument issued to him or her is the only one that can be played. Let's look at some of the major elements of the inner life of the associate, with initial attention on character issues and later the personality. How is the inner life important for the creation of beautiful music from the church staff?

Guard Your Heart

At the center of character is the heart. Solomon tells us, "Above all else, guard your heart, for it is the wellspring of life" (Prov. 4:23). The heart or soul is that intangible inner person and is to be guarded jealously. In a direct way, the heart provides a vital source of direction

35

and motivation for the ministry of the associate. Guarding the inner person is protecting the instrument that God has given the associate to play on the church staff.

One way to guard your heart is to practice those disciplines that develop the qualities of an elder or pastor listed in 1 Timothy 3:1–7 and Titus 1:7–9. The combined list includes being above reproach (blameless), the husband of one wife, temperate, self-controlled, respectable, hospitable, able to teach, not given to drunkenness, not violent but gentle, not quarrelsome, not a lover of money, manager of own family, one who sees that the children obey with proper respect, not a recent convert, of good reputation with outsiders, not overbearing, not quick tempered, not pursuing dishonest gain, one who loves what is good, is upright, is holy, is disciplined, and who holds firmly to the trustworthy message as it has been taught so that he can encourage others by sound doctrine and refute those who oppose it.

These qualities listed in these two passages relate to a person's character and are primarily inner. There are outward manifestations of the inner qualities, but the inner life is not measured by typical methods. Normal measurements of these qualities are proxies for the real thing. For example, the type of educational degree a person holds and the place from which it was earned usually engenders a set of assumptions about that person. Nothing whatever, though, is directly said about education—formal or informal—in the scriptural list. Most churches give practical experience great emphasis in determining the inner qualities of an associate, but aside from not being a recent convert, nothing is directly mentioned about experience in ministry. The qualities in Scripture can be explained in those who have previous ministry experience, but more often than not, the experience serves as a proxy for the scriptural qualities. Proxies seldom indicate what one thinks they do, however.

Why are these qualities so difficult to determine? Why are the qualities of the inner life avoided when evaluating a candidate? Is it because a definitive answer regarding the qualities of the inner life is so difficult to determine? Is it because the interviewer is fearful that he will be measured by the same standard? If an honest answer about each of these qualities were received from the potential associate, would and could the answer be believed? If others who were friends of the potential associate were queried as to their opinions, could their views be trusted as being without bias? These and other issues should not deter inquiry into these inner qualities. Far too much is at stake to make assumptions that may prove to be disastrous, because an associate with an unguarded heart will have an unprotected instrument.

Walk in the Word

Consider this question: Does serving God full-time as an associate pastor insure that there will be a vital, growing, and exciting walk with God and his Word in the associate's life? My own experience and that of other associates I know has lead me to believe the answer to this question is negative. The pastoral ministry tends to draw one away from a vital and dynamic walk with God because it is easy to substitute professional preparation for the devotional feeding of your soul. With the press of duties, professional preparation usually takes precedence over devotional preparation. One has to struggle to maintain a personal walk with Christ in His Word while ministering to the needs of others.

Seeking spiritual sustenance from the spiritual spade work of others will not provide lasting or sufficient spiritual food for a minister of the Gospel. Public meetings, tapes of messages, or even written devotional thoughts of others cannot alone nurture the continual spiritual growth of the associate as can the Spirit of God in and through personal, devotional, and intense study of God's Word.

Corporate worship is important in the Christian life, but should not be a substitute for the associate's personal walk with Christ. Worship with other believers is necessary and significant, but cannot replace that private time with God in his word. If the duties of the associate do not allow participation in corporate worship, alternative worship times with other believers should be sought. It should be kept in mind that the preaching of someone else (or even yourself) cannot replace God's Spirit that is speaking to you through his Word. The associate must take personal responsibility for being a self-feeder. The process of maturing in Christ happens in no other way. Nourishing one's self on the Word of God must be a daily habit for the growing associate.

Psalm 119 is filled with admonitions concerning God's Word and a holy walk. Verse 9 asks, "How can a young man keep his way pure? By living according to your word." Verse 105 states, "Your word is a lamp to my feet and a light for my path." Verse 104 says, "I gain understanding from your precepts; therefore I hate every wrong path." God's Word must have a dominant place in the life of an associate.

Walk in the Spirit

Should a vital, growing, and exciting life in the Spirit of God be required of the one who desires to serve as an associate pastor? This *should* be true, but often it isn't. The reason is that so much is assumed about the associate that may not be true at all. To assume without verification that a vital, robust, personal, Spirit-filled walk with Christ exists as an integral part of the character of any potential pastor may be a serious mistake. Degrees from a school or ministry experience do not create or guarantee such a walk. Assuming that such a walk with Christ is present when it is not could be catastrophic to the church, the unsaved, the other members of the staff, those ministered to, and the associate.

Consider the alternative. If an associate is not walking with God in the power of the Spirit of God, then what power or strength is being used to serve? Serving Christ in the power of one's flesh is not only warned against in Scripture (Gal. 5:16–26) it is contradictory to attempt it. Paul said, "For the sinful nature desires what is contrary to the Spirit, and the Spirit what is contrary to the sinful nature" (17a). The attempt to do God's work with fleshly weapons is futile. Only frustration and ineffectual service will result from fleshly service. "The weapons we fight with are not the weapons of the world. On the contrary, they have divine power to demolish strongholds" (2 Cor. 10:4). It is "not by might nor by power, but by my Spirit, says the LORD Almighty" (Zech. 4:6).

Knowing the facts about walking in the Spirit will not make it happen in the associate's life. Knowing the facts and not doing it is sin (see James 4:17). The reading of this chapter may be producing a sense of guilt in those who know perfectly well what they should be doing but find it difficult (if not impossible) to do. The ideal of being led by the Spirit has often been replaced by the crunch of too many urgent ministry requests. The life of the associate must center on a consistent walk with the Spirit and a rich relationship with the Savior, thereby nourishing the associate's instrument.

Prayer

What has been said about the importance of Bible study and walking in the Spirit also applies to the importance of prayer. What Christian minister would say they pray enough? How much prayer is enough for one committed to serving God with his life and in his vocation? Is the prayer of the professional minister always an expression of personal dependence on God?

A distinction should be made here between formal and informal prayer. All believers are told to pray without ceasing (1 Thess. 5:17). Obviously to pray continually in a formal sense would interfere with the many other duties of our lives. But praying informally is an attitude of dependence on God for the decisions of every moment. Praying unceasingly while remaining informal is not as easy as it may appear. One way to measure the level of unceasing prayer is to ask yourself, "What is my first thought when faced with life's emergencies?"

Is there a conscious dependence on God, or a dependence on wit, skill, knowledge, or fleshly strength? Scripture also says to "Be anxious for nothing, but in everything by prayer and supplication with thanksgiving let your requests be made known to God" (Phil. 4:6 NASB). More than how many hours are spent in prayer, the question should be, When the time of crisis comes, on whom (better on Whom) does the associate depend? What is the direction of our first thoughts? To God or to how we can solve our own problem? Prayer is as vital to a relationship with God as breathing is to physical life. Unceasing prayer is vital to the life of the associate.

Integrity

The issue of integrity is certainly central to the associate's character. Reputation is what is seen in the light, integrity is what happens in the dark. Integrity is being honest when no one is looking, honorable when it does not seem to matter, and acting on principle when everyone around you wants to do what is expedient. Integrity is very important to the life of the associate, and like other elements of character, it seems we don't know how to evaluate if someone has it or not. It is possible, however, to recognize it.

A pastor I knew told me about his adult, but unmarried, child who had terribly disappointed him. This son was financially supported by some of the pastor's church members through a mission organization in which the son served. The pastor told me that he planned to read a letter to the whole congregation that explained what had happened with his son. He would first explain everything and then explain what steps were being taken to correct the situation. I told him I thought he should tell the elders and send the letter only to those in the church who supported his son, saying nothing to the whole congregation. I expected that telling the whole congregation would cause the church to blame him and call for his resignation. I was wrong.

He chose to read the letter to the whole congregation and did so the following Sunday. Instead of calling for his resignation because he had not controlled his own household, the congregation supported the pastor, his wife, and his son. They agreed to assist in the reconciliation process of the son. They applauded the pastor's integrity in telling the whole truth, even though it tore his heart out to do it.

In another situation, a pastor with whom I served revealed an appalling lack of integrity. At the time I interviewed, this pastor had served the same church for two decades, and I asked about his plans for the future. He said that he "did not know how God would lead him." Three months after I arrived, he presented his resignation as pastor of the church. He was not being called to another church but said he probably would leave the ministry. I was left as the only pastoral staff member in the church of about 650 members.

About a year after the pastor resigned, he divorced his wife of twenty-five years and quickly married a woman from the same church he had pastored. It was clear to me that he had planned this series of events for years because it had become known that he had been having an eight-year affair with this woman. He waited to divorce and remarry until his youngest child was old enough not to require child support. He rationalized his behavior by saying he believed God wanted him to be happy. He needed an ordained associate to whom he could turn over his church responsibilities and I was that person. I was not the only one who felt betrayed. Integrity can often be recognized by its absence. Psalm 15 is a good summary of integrity.

> Lord, who may dwell in your sanctuary?
>   Who may live on your holy hill?
> He whose walk is blameless,
>   and who does what is righteous,
> who speaks the truth from his heart
>   and has no slander on his tongue,
> who does his neighbor no wrong
>   and casts no slur on his fellowman,
> who despises a vile man
>   but honors those who fear the Lord,
> who keeps his oath
>   even when it hurts,
> who lends his money without usury
>   and does not accept a bribe against the innocent.
> He who does these things
>   will never be shaken.

Accountability

A counterpart to integrity in the character of the associate is the ability to be accountable to someone else. It is curious to me that we treat accountability with a human differently than we treat accountability with God. While it is true we can tell God that we will follow through with some aspect of commitment, it is also true that we (at least I) find it easy to excuse ourselves to God. After all, God is merciful and loving. He will understand my frailty and inability to follow through as I promised. I find it much harder to tell a human being that I did not follow through. Why is that? Do I fear a human being more than God? I don't believe I fear a human more than God, but there may be other reasons that human accountability works better. A human provides more immediate feedback on the request and can inquire about the specifics of my commitment. Other people may also be accountable to me; therefore the process has mutual benefit. Whatever the reason for this difference, we can use this phenomenon to improve our accountability.

Sharing the inner workings of one's life is not always easy, even with someone you know. It is especially difficult to be transparent with your supervisor because you know that your job security may depend on what you say. We don't want to be burned (as perhaps we have been in the past), so we learn how to play games. When asked for a personal accountability item, we offer something rather innocuous, simple, or nonthreatening to us. The heart-rending situations we keep to ourselves.

David Smith, in his book, *The Friendless American Male*, describes the sharing problem most men in our culture face. He describes three types of friends—acquaintance, companion, and intimate. The first is by far the most numerous because we know only a little about acquaintances, such as name, vocation, family size, perhaps names of some of the children, the model of car driven, and not much else. The companion may share a common interest, such as a sport or a hobby. You know more about a companion but not what he feels about a wide variety of subjects. The intimate friend is someone you can tell anything to, and you know he will still be your friend. Smith declares that most American men do not have the intimate kind of friendship.[1] This reality includes pastors and their associates, also.

It takes a long time to build up a high level of trust in an accountability relationship. When the simple things are resolved, deeper-level things can be shared. The process continues, and hopefully, an intimate level of relationship is achieved among the staff. Games will no longer be played, and, over time, a deep and mature relationship will emerge.

One pastor with whom I shared ministry was in his fortieth year of ministry when I came to work with him. He had worked with a great number of associate staff in his ministry. From his remarks about them, I concluded that none of them had lived up to his expectations. I did not want my name added to the list. My immediate predecessor had been criticized for having another full-time job. Another predecessor was derided because she had not done some assigned task. An open level of sharing with this pastor took at least three years to develop. I was continually being evaluated by the standards set by my predecessors. A high level of trust between the senior pastor and myself finally developed only after I consistently demonstrated that

41

he could trust me—at first in the small things, such as the repair of an office machine, and then later, in praying with him about a personal problem.

What associate would not thrill to be a part of a caring and supportive relationship with others on a church staff? It is possible. It is also necessary. How many churches have observed a church staff that demonstrates genuine *koinonia?* When members of the church staff bicker with each other privately or publicly, it destroys the very concepts they may be teaching. Everyone on the church staff should be called to the same standard of unity and brotherly love they preach and teach so loud and long. It is the only way for beautiful music to emerge.

Personality

In addition to character, the associate who understands the kind of personality God has given to him or her is far better suited to meet the unique demands of serving on the pastoral staff. Examining every aspect of a person's personality is far beyond the scope of this book, but there are some aspects that can be helpful for the associate pastor to know. If a person knows his or her own instrument, it helps in finding the right fit in the pastoral ensemble.

Most personality inventories are secular in orientation and are meant to be used independent of any other instrument. I have found a technique that sheds light on specific types of personality and matches each type with various spiritual gifts.[2] This inventory combines the DiSC™ Profile and a spiritual-gift inventory. The results of each are combined to supply descriptions of several personality types. The implications are fascinating when two or more of the combined types serve on a pastoral staff.

The four personality types follow the four letters of DiSC™ with *D* standing for dominant. The letter *I* is for influencing, and *S* and *C* for steady and compliant. Those who are *D* and *I* are active and outgoing, whereas *S* and *C* are more reserved and passive. In addition, those who are *D* and *C* are more task oriented, and *I* and *S* more people oriented.[3] With an awareness of which personality types combine with which spiritual gifts, relationships on the church staff take on new dimensions.

Consider, for example, the interaction between a high-*D* staff person with the gift of exhortation, and another high-*D* with the gift of administration. Since both are dominant personality types, conflicts between the two are inevitable. If the *D* with exhortation is the senior pastor and the other person is a staff member, the conflicts will probably center on the ways in which each person is failing to fulfill the functions that are important to the other. The exhorter will exhort the administrator to exhort more and the administrator will admonish the other for some administrative failure. Since they are both *D*'s, the conflict may be continual. If they do not recognize why they argue and disagree, beautiful music from them is unlikely.

Persistence

A personality trait that is related to personality type is persistence. The *D* with the gift of administration is task oriented but cares little for details. This *D* prefers the big picture and wants to set a vision. It is the *C* with the gift of administration who enjoys following up on the organizational detail required to execute a vision that is not necessarily his own. Every personality type can be persistent, but the persons who are either *S* or *C* will shine when it comes to persistence in the assigned tasks. The *S* is steady and careful and the *C* is cautious and conscientious. If persistence is important to the effectiveness of the associate, it is easier for some personality types to fulfill this expectation.

Peter says in his second letter that believers should "make every effort to add to your faith goodness; and to goodness, knowledge; and to knowledge, self-control; and to self-control, perseverance . . ." (2 Peter 1:5–6). He goes on to say that "if you possess these qualities in increasing measure, they will help you from being ineffective and unproductive in your knowledge of our Lord Jesus Christ" (2 Peter 1:8). Persistence always enhances the ministry of the associate.

It should be noted that there must be a balance between being persistent and overworking. Being a workaholic benefits no one. Doing more work than you should deprives others from sharing in the ministry. Long hours contribute to the breakdown of family unity and togetherness. Persistence to the task is fine, but obsessive overwork is shortsighted and not in the best interests of the ministry or the associate. More will be said about overwork later, but a balance is necessary in the associate's life.

Goal Oriented

A trait related to persistence, but an important separate issue, is the ability to set and achieve goals. Paul referred to his ministry when he said, "I press on toward the goal to win the prize for which God has called me heavenward in Christ Jesus" (Phil. 3:14). Different personalities treat goal setting in diverse ways. Before we get into that, it may help to define what a goal is, what kind of outcome it represents.

Goals can be thought of as segments of larger, less measurable purposes. Whereas there might be few purposes of a church, or perhaps only one, there could be several major goals. An objective is a measurable outcome that is based on a goal. There are many objectives that are usually related to church programs. Associates are often assigned the responsibility for some of these programs.

For example, a purpose of a church might be to bring all believers to spiritual maturity. This purpose is large and as stated, unmeasurable. While everyone may agree with it, specific strategies to achieve it are unclear. A goal to assist the achievement of this purpose might be to develop consistent Bible study in every believer. There are various kinds of goals and cultivating spiritual maturity is a skill or behavioral goal.[4] An objective for this goal could be to implement the use of graded, inductive Bible study skills for all Sunday school students during the next year from the seventh grade through the adult classes. The objective should be written so it can be measured within a set period of time. Objectives should be graded for each group so that each can achieve the objectives appropriate to their maturity level. When evaluation time comes, it should be clear if the objective was reached. If not, a new objective and strategy can be formulated based on new information.

One important reason the associate must be skilled in goal setting and achievement is because goals (and objectives) will be used to evaluate his or her work. If the associate does not take the initiative in setting goals because of personality type, evaluation will be based on the goals of other people, primarily the supervisors. It is far better to be evaluated on the basis of goals you set yourself than on the goals others set for you. Setting goals is only the beginning; communicating them to others and then working to achieve them through the objectives are also crucial. How many associates have found out too late that their service was weighed and found wanting? This is not to say that if a personality type does not prefer to set goals that the person is thereby relieved of that task. It does not mean that by any means. It does mean that if a high *D* associate is responsible for administrative detail, in order for that associate to continue in that ministry, someone must be recruited who can step in and provide that service, preferably a high *C*. This is where the skill of negotiation enters.

Negotiation

One of the most important skills of an associate is the ability to negotiate. The ability to negotiate is probably based on a humble attitude about one's self-importance. Paul tells us: "Do nothing out of selfish ambition or vain conceit, but in humility consider others better than yourselves" (Phil. 2:3). One of the results of advanced training and years of experience is the creation of a certain level of expertise. One can be confident in one's abilities, but when confidence crosses over into pride, one effect is stubbornness when negotiating. It is easy to think you are right when no one else has the level of education and experience in the area to which you have been assigned. Giving in, finding common ground, yielding to other points of view are crucial skills for an associate to possess. These skills are, in large measure, a consequence of the personality type and spiritual gift.

Take the role of negotiation in regard to planning, as it affects a church staff. Proverbs tells us that "plans fail for lack of counsel, but with many advisers they succeed" (15:22). How many opinions are there in a group of five people? The answer is at least five and perhaps many more. The key to successful group work is not forcing your opinion on others but negotiating a path through the many opinions that all group members will embrace, own, and help to fulfill.

The associate who is a high *I* with the gift of exhortation or teaching will try to persuade the group to accept his or her opinion and interpret what is done as leadership. An associate who is a high *S* with the gift of helps will certainly negotiate differently and probably get different results. If everyone on the church staff understood the other members in this way, would not the expression of personal opinion more likely proceed without becoming antagonistic or hostile?

Some situations may require the associate to wait for the right time to express an opinion. I told one pastor (a high *D* with the gift of exhortation) with whom I served on a church staff that outside our staff meetings I would support him fully, especially before members of the congregation. I (a high *C* with the gifts of administration and teaching) expressed the hope that he would do the same for me, and he assured me he would. I added that I hoped that inside the staff meeting we could express any opinion without fear of becoming fodder for church gossip. In other words, in the staff meeting, anything went. Outside the staff meeting, the staff was united and supportive of one another. High *D*'s are straightforward and blunt and like to relate to others in this way. The agreement we struck that day was one of the finest ground rules for high-quality negotiation I could have suggested. Ideas and plans for programs, events, and responses to situations were negotiated in a straightforward and open fashion. So much more was accomplished because negotiation between the parties was based on personality types and preferences.

Handling Criticism

Another issue related to personality type is the ability to handle criticism. Proverbs tells us that "a gentle answer turns away wrath, but a harsh word stirs up anger" (15:1). Anyone who has served in the church knows the value of a gentle answer. Criticism comes to the associate veiled as concern, curiosity, or other euphemistic terms, but it all hurts the same. Michael Woodruff gives six excellent pieces of advice to youth associates regarding criticism. He says to (1) expect criticism, (2) assume criticism is valid until proven otherwise, (3) delay your response to criticism, (4) request criticism, (5) demand evenhanded criticism, and (6) realize that sometimes criticism is just part of the system.[5]

It is often said that developing a thick skin is a helpful attribute for the ministry. I would like to suggest that how we respond to criticism relates to personality. The high D will more easily brush off criticism than the high S. Either of the types who value greatly what others think of them (I and S with the gift of mercy) will find it much more difficult to develop a rhinolike hide. The ability to discard negative comments does not come easily to those who are more sensitive to what others think of them. Being sensitive to others should be one of the characteristics of a minister, but separating your sensitivity to others from being sensitive to what others say about you is not easily accomplished for certain personality types.

I suppose the ability to handle the darts and barbs from others has to do more with the associate's self-esteem than the actual shortcoming being discussed. A healthy self-esteem would certainly help the sensitive associate pastor to weather the storms of criticism that arise. Healthy self-esteem recognizes that each person is a unique creation of a loving God who has created us for good works (Eph. 2:10). At the same time, believers are urged to have the same attitude as Jesus Christ who made himself nothing and took the nature of a servant (Phil. 2:5–7). This balance between these two elements is significant for the self-esteem of an associate.

If a person seeks to please others to an extreme degree, his or her well-being will depend on the positive reinforcement he or she receives. People-oriented personalities (I and S) will find that the smallest amount of criticism can send them into a tailspin. A high D or C would probably not take the criticism as seriously. Praise and appreciation for all types of people are far more effective than criticism in helping change to occur. Knowing this, I find it amazing that pointing out the imperfections of the members of the church staff is so popular and easy to do. Understanding your instrument helps you respond with beautiful music when (not if) you are criticized.

Work Level

Every associate realizes sooner or later that the ministry in which he or she serves is a big job that does not seem ever to be finished. Working nonstop would certainly help to address the needs of the ministry, but that is not possible. What level of work is appropriate for an associate? I suggest that the way in which an associate sets the work level is an expression of personality type and spiritual gift. Do persons with different personality types and spiritual-gift packages view the demands of ministry in the same way? Do these different people go about work in the same way? How would these differences affect the associate?

The two types of personalities on the DiSC™ profile that are work oriented are *D* and *C*. The other two, *I* and *S* are more people oriented. It would seem that the work-oriented pair would tend toward workaholism more than the other pair. It is conceivable that *D* and *C* could possess a higher work level; it is possible that *I* and *S* could also be workaholics but for different reasons. Those gifted as administrators should be able to organize their time efficiently, and those gifted with mercy might find themselves overwhelmed with the concerns of people. The type of personality and specific spiritual gifts will affect the level of work. Can we accept the differences of others and allow them to function at a level that is comfortable for them?

Everyone will be revived by different activities or some by no activity at all. The associate must be known for making regular rest a priority. One should not be legalistic about the day off, but it should not be regularly overruled by the demands of ministry. Workaholic associates may be appreciated by some in the church, but more thoughtful observers will expect the associate to regularly take time for renewal and refreshment. They know such an associate will be a better servant in the long run than one who is on a path of self-destruction.

In spite of the personality and gift package, it is the senior pastor who often leads by example as one addicted to work. If the associate fails to put in as many hours as the senior pastor, the contrast becomes obvious. Casual references to the length of one's work week are noticed and comparisons are made. It is the senior pastor who must lead the way by taking time for regular recreation because associates will find it difficult to do so without his example. The associate might be the one working long hours and the senior may feel threatened thereby, but usually the senior is the one who overworks. Recreation is needed by all to allow for the necessary care of the minister's instrument.

An important element in determining the work level is the ability to say no—without guilt. How do you respond to the telephone call on your day off? It is usually a question or requires you to make a decision. It may even require you to go to another location and take care of something you forgot. It may be something that the caller thinks cannot wait until another day. Can you say no to the request? If you can, can you do it without guilt?

The impact of these types of requests is most noticed on the day off, but the root of the problem often lies in the associate's view of the ministry. Both the work-oriented and the people-oriented associate may find it very hard to say no to a request within their respective orientation. For example, if a person brings a request to a high *D* or *C*, a yes or no will depend on whether or not it fits into the ministry description and goals. If it does not, it is easier for the associate to decline without guilt. The associate with the gift of administration, exhortation, teaching, or prophecy will find it easy to explain why he or she cannot help the caller.

If the caller has a request for a high *I* or *S*, the answer will depend more on personal relationship than ministry description or goals. Those associates with the spiritual gifts of mercy, helps, and the like will evaluate how much damage to the personal relationship with this person or family would result by saying no. If the request is declined, the person may feel offended or, worse, may complain to the senior pastor or official board members. Now the guilt potential has risen dramatically. Responding properly often depends on understanding ourselves and why we respond to people's requests as we do.

Conclusion

These are some of the issues related to the maintenance of the instrument the associate has been given. It is necessary to care for it and see to it that the character and personality of the associate be kept in excellent condition. The music made by the church staff will suffer if no one watches and cares for the character of or understands the personality and spiritual gifts of the associate.

Discussion Questions

Use these questions privately or in a group, such as a church staff, to apply the points made in this chapter.

1. What does it mean to you personally to guard your heart?

2. How consistent is your personal Bible study?

3. How meaningful is your personal Bible study?

4. What evidence can you cite that you are walking in the Spirit?

5. Is your dependence on God obvious from your first reaction to a crisis?

6. Are you a persistent person? How do you know that you are or are not?

7. Do you set goals and objectives for yourself that are measurable and achievable? If yes, name one you are working on presently. If no, write out some goals and objectives.

8. When confronted by someone who disagrees with you, how do you normally react? How good are you at negotiation?

9. What is the current shape of your self-esteem, as seen by your response to criticism?

10. What example can you cite that demonstrates the presence of integrity in your life?

11. What example can you cite that demonstrates the absence of integrity in your life?

12. What kind of friend are you to those in an accountability relationship?

13. Do you play accountability games? Do others on your staff? If so, why?

14. With whom are you vulnerable? Do you have someone whom you would call an intimate friend?

15. Do you take regular time off to refresh yourself? If not, why not?

16. Have you developed the ability to say no without guilt? If so, how do you do it?

Part 2:

Role Expectations

CHAPTER FOUR

What Does the Church
Want to Hear?
(Expectations of the Church)

I believe it was and is God's intention for beautiful music to flow from church-staff relationships. An important element to harmonious church-staff relationships is expectation. Sources of expectations vary and come from associates themselves, from the official church board, and from the church in general. Let's begin with the expectations for the associate by the church in general and how these might affect the harmony of church-staff relationships.

Church Covenant

I have observed in each church that I have served a general set of expectations that affect the associate as well as everyone in the congregation. This set of expectations I have called a "covenant." I am not referring simply to the written document by that name that some churches present to new members. I am referring to a broader set of expectations, such as an ethos, that each church employs to function. The covenant may have written elements, but more importantly, there are also unwritten elements, those assumptions and expectations that the church applies in its operation.

A covenant includes what the church will offer potential members, such as what their beliefs are, and the various religious activities and services that will be offered. The covenant also includes what is expected from each person who desires membership in that particular church. Parts of this covenant are usually described during new-member orientation. Other parts are learned as time goes by and more experience with the church occurs. The covenant is agreed on by those present when the church is founded, sometimes after intensive work over a period of time or sometimes after a slow and unintentional evolution.

Churches have found that a covenant that places limited demands on potential members will draw more persons into its fellowship. Such a covenant requires less commitment, less time, and requests less money. In short, it is a "lite" church. Some of these lite churches have no official membership at all. The opposite kind of church is the legalistic church with explicit and heavy responsibilities placed on those who have chosen to become members. The legalistic church will usually draw members more slowly at first, but the members will usually exhibit a higher quality of commitment to the church.

The church with a limited covenant may encounter difficulties as it develops. The lite church will encounter recruitment difficulties when staffing needs for desired programs cannot be filled with the few volunteer workers. A crisis may be perceived in the lite church when the congregation is informed that the original covenant no longer is adequate and has to be changed. This proposed change may cause people to leave the church, cause a church split, or cause some to call for the resignation of the pastor and/or staff members.

The legalistic church with its high demands on people could face its own type of crisis—the burnout of its workers. If the church is built on new believers, initial enthusiasm will be high, but may not last. As awareness arises of what other churches require, dissatisfaction may grow, workers may resign, openings may go unfilled. Criticism of those not fully serving will create disunity and possibly a church split. There may be a call for resignations in this type of church as well, although it is not as likely as in the church with the minimal covenant.

Newcomers to a church body may come from another church (transfer) or from no church at all (new believers). The new believers will likely have little or no church experience in their background and will have little trouble accepting uncritically the requirements of the covenant. For example, if the new believers are told believers will tithe their income to the church, attend every activity of the church, and serve in at least one church program, they will usually comply. They have no religious experience with which to compare the requirements. Transfers from other churches are not normally so willing to accept the same terms.

The transfer-type newcomer has other church experience with which to compare the covenant of the new church. What the new church expects from new members will be compared with the person's experience in all previous churches. For example, if there is a heavy emphasis placed on each member's serving according to spiritual gifts in the new church, this may not be well received by the transfer newcomer. This type of newcomer might be burned-out from service and may be seeking to "hide" in the new church, especially if it is larger than their former one. The transfer newcomer may observe the current members of the new church and conclude that not everyone is serving. The push for service in the new-member's class is unenforced rhetoric and meaningless. This observation may allow the transfer newcomer freedom to join the church without fulfilling that part of the covenant and doing so without guilt. The new-believer newcomers can make the same observations about the church, but that usually will not prevent them from signing up to serve in a church program. They may be too naive at first to decline to serve.

Pastor Rick Warren said that when Saddleback Community Church was beginning, they would give positions of leadership to "any warm body." After the church was established and the organization more complex, the requirements for workers became stiffer and stiffer. The covenant shifted from lite to heavy over a period of time. Qualifications also become stiffer for lay pastors, musicians, and other ministry positions.[1] If a church is experiencing trouble finding people willing to serve in the church, it may be due to the covenant. Those who are untrained are more willing to serve, but the trained and experienced workers soon discover that they can decline to serve and no one will think the less of them. The willing and untrained can be trained, of course, if there is sufficient leadership to do so. Unfortunately, there often is not.

How the church covenant affects the associate is interesting. If one of the functions of an associate pastor is to enlist and train workers in the church for any of its programs, the church covenant regarding service must be completely understood. Is the official church policy of Christian service effectively implemented? It is easy to have a written policy for every member's involvement in service, but is every member actually serving? If the answer is no, then the official covenant is contradicted by the actual covenant. This obvious contradiction will make the task of any person who is responsible for recruitment (usually the associate) all the more difficult.

A thorough understanding of the church's covenant in relationship to its members may not be possible in a brief interview between a search committee and a candidate. It may take some time to discern the actual covenant of a church (especially the unwritten elements), but knowing how the covenant actually functions is crucial for the effective service of the candidate who will serve as an associate pastor. The candidate must ask pointed questions of the appropriate people and must receive honest answers in order for the associate to have the information necessary to make an intelligent decision about accepting the call of the church. The covenant is a key element of church tradition for associates.

I have found that the covenant of any church I have served was well understood by the members of the church, but it took "newbies" (myself included) some time to understand it and learn how to work with it. One church I served expected three hours or more on Sunday morning, one and one-half to two hours on Sunday night and the same on Wednesday night. Another church I served expected that one and a half hours was the limit of the Sunday morning commitment. The length of the service was ninety minutes and a Sunday school for children and youth ran concurrently with the worship service. When the adults were asked to teach Sunday school, it conflicted with attendance at worship service. In order to teach, the worship service would have to be missed.

Even though there were two identical worship services, and two identical Sunday schools, the covenant of ninety minutes would not be violated. Almost the entire church thought it was inconceivable that teachers would attend both sessions, teaching in one and worshiping in the other. A commitment of three and one-half hours (including a thirty-minute break between services) was not in the (unwritten) covenant and would not be accepted. The Sunday school would have to go without the necessary teachers. The covenant of the church triumphed over the needs of a program that many people said they wanted.

Vague or Specific

In one of the churches I served, I was called as an associate pastor, and my title was Minister of Education. I was given a detailed description of job duties, which was a little over three single-spaced pages in length. Every conceivable activity of Christian education was listed, including the planning, enlisting, training, and supervising for every kind of educational program for all age groups. In short, I was responsible for everything that had anything to do with Christian education in that church.

In this detailed list of duties were the typical ones, including Sunday school and youth ministries. There was also a description of a specific children's club program, one for boys and one for girls, that the church did not have at the time nor had ever had at anytime in its history. When interviewing, I asked if these clubs were planned for the future. The pastor told me that the church did not have those programs at the time and had no plans to begin them anytime soon. If, however, they were deemed necessary at a later date, I would be in charge of them.

When I was asked several years later to organize the new visitation evangelism program, I recalled that this program was not on my list of duties. Before I could point this out to the pastor, I was surprised when the senior pastor pointed out to me that this new responsibility would take the place of the children's clubs that were on my job description but were not being done. He reasoned that there should be time in my schedule to do the evangelism program since the specific children's clubs were not being conducted. I guess he forgot the alternative program running on Wednesday night for children (as well as for youth and adults) that served the same purpose as the children's clubs described in my ministry description. The Wednesday night program, as it was being conducted, did not appear on my ministry description either, but it was being done. It appeared that the incredibly detailed job description still needed something added to it.

In another church that I examined with the possibility of serving there, I was given a description of duties for a director of Christian education that lacked any detail at all. Vague allusions to "all Christian education functions" had no specific duties or age groups listed. My reaction after reading this description was that the people who wrote it either were unsure of what a director of Christian education did or perhaps expected the new director of Christian education to shape the job description after arrival. So, which type of description is best? The answer is, that depends. Let's explore some of the things on which it depends.

First of all, no ministry description grows out of a vacuum. In the first case described above, the detailed description of expectations was developed because my predecessor had not fulfilled the expectations of his rather vague ministry description. The pastor was not going to allow that to happen again. If my predecessor had been successful in fulfilling the general expectations listed on his job description there probably would not have been an extremely detailed version created for me. If the predecessor's ministry was considered "successful" or effective, the ministry expectations for his successor would have been vague and general also. The senior pastor felt he needed to protect himself and the church by creating the detailed job description.

Associate ministers, right from the beginning, often experience confusion regarding the description of the proposed ministry. In other situations, the description of the associate position seems rather clear and straightforward, but most members of the congregation do not seem to fully understand it. These parishioners will have no idea of what is specifically written or expected from the person filling the role of associate pastor. Even if the search committee verbalizes a written list of obvious expectations, their hidden agenda may involve unwritten ones that are not clear and perhaps not even discussed among themselves or the candidate. More about that later.

The general title, Associate Pastor, is a catchall term that encompasses any and all expectations from the senior pastor and the congregation. If there are no other pastoral staff members (as in a smaller church), the associate might be given responsibilities for many things. This list might include Christian education, including the entire Sunday school; special activities for children, youth, and adults; pastoral duties, such as substitute preaching, visitation, and counseling; music leading (if so talented); worship planning; outreach ministries, such as small groups, new-member classes, and family ministries; church administration, including budget monitoring, facilities maintenance, as well as secretarial and janitorial supervision and/or duties; teaching a class in any of the church agencies; and any other duties that the pastor may require.

It is no wonder that a general associate may feel frustrated and unfulfilled. In some cases, the job description may be manageable. However, frustration may set in as the list continues to expand in an uncontrollable fashion. The new duties may not interest the associate or may require the use of spiritual gifts and abilities he or she does not possess. This is particularly true if the ministry description is large in its scope and the time and pay are for part-time work. Most anyone would feel overwhelmed by a list as diverse as some that are posed to associate candidates. It would require a person of multiple gifts and talents to satisfactorily fulfill all the required duties, and not everyone is so endowed.

Should the ministry description be detailed, leaving very little to interpretation, expansion, or omission? Or should the ministry description be general and vague so there is great latitude and flexibility? Both have appropriate applications in a church with an associate, but it seems as if both should be carefully considered and negotiated if the associate and the church body are to produce beautiful music.

Ministry descriptions will change over time, so which comes first, the ministry description or getting to know the strengths and weaknesses of the new associate? Don't pastoral-staff members shift the focus of their interest as they mature and grow older? Did the congregation know all the talents and abilities of the associate immediately upon his or her arrival? What about other members of the staff who leave, thus making a new configuration of staff responsibilities possible and perhaps necessary? Can the church shift ministry descriptions without forcing an associate to resign or move on?

These possibilities show us that no ministry description for a pastoral associate comes out of a void. There is always a reason that the ministry description takes a specific shape, and it is important to understand that reason. I can say that my experience with both general and specific descriptions was positive and happy because I was accepted for who I was, not as the committee's idealized concept of an associate pastor.

The key issue in ministry descriptions is not only just the amount of detail but also the trust between the principal parties involved. If you feel more comfortable with a detailed description of duties, then be sure to ask for more explanation. If you are fearful of so much detail, ask about how you will be evaluated. If you are a pastor or search-committee member, be sure to ask each candidate what he or she feels most comfortable with, and design the ministry description accordingly. In the process, the following questions might be used: Are the persons who are primarily involved in this enterprise people of integrity? Is the description detailed because the senior pastor is only interested in holding the associate's "feet to the fire"? Or is the senior pastor more interested in seeing general progress in the areas of assigned responsibility? Is the pastor looking for signs of personal development and growth, or does he simply want the various jobs to be done to his satisfaction?

Understanding how all parties view the written ministry description is vital to living comfortably with it. If the written document is to be viewed in a literal and wooden fashion, then effectiveness will probably be measured in quantitative ways: Did your group have more attendance this week than the week before? If the written document is viewed as a general guide and beacon for the journey ahead, then evaluation is probably going to be more qualitative: Is there enthusiastic support for the ministry you are doing?

One thing is sure—the associate will be evaluated. There is no doubt about that. It is crucial, however, that all parties involved—the senior pastor, the associate, church leaders, and church members—be aware of what will be evaluated, when the evaluation will occur, and how the evaluation will occur. Items that refer to evaluation can be included in the ministry description. This will help to provide a measure of accountability. A time frame for evaluations can also be included in the ministry description. There is little benefit to the church or the associate in being evaluated for expectations that are unknown or unanticipated.

Part- or Full-Time

The associate who is appointed as full time may be operating under the delusion that the work week is limited to forty hours. One pastor I worked with told me he did not care how much time I took to fulfill my duties, as long as the job got done. While that sounded great at first, I later realized it took far more than forty hours a week to complete the many assigned tasks to his satisfaction. If it is expected that actual hours worked are to be recorded and reported to the associate's supervisor, a large number of hours per week will likely have contrasting effects, delighting the supervisor and discouraging the associate.

The part-time associate may be limited to a certain number of hours per week to complete his ministry responsibilities. Dividing the part-timer's pay by the number of hours will reveal the rate of pay. When the number of hours increases and the pay remains the same, the part-time associate wonders if he or she is being taken advantage of by the church. Many associates who are just starting out, want to do well for the sake of a good recommendation. This makes them invest more hours than the required minimum and can lead to burnout.

When the written expectations of the church for the associate exceed the maximum number of hours to accomplish them, the associate has a problem. It may not even be clear to the associate at first that there is a potential problem. The lack of ministry experience shields them from understanding how their duties will actually be accomplished. Even full-time associates can run into this problem. Can they actually put in the amount of time necessary to fulfill their ministry responsibilities to everyone's satisfaction? Can they afford to be gone so many evenings and weekends from their families? The terms *part time* and *full time* must be clearly defined in regard to the duties expected as well as in regard to number of hours invested.

Some associates—due to spiritual gifts, experience, or natural skills—can fulfill a duty in less time or with less effort than it might take another associate who lacks those qualities. Defining a ministry by the amount of time expected for each duty will not be an appropriate measure. Those who work quickly can be given more duties and those who work more slowly may need their duties pared back, at least for a while. Shaping the ministry description to the individual associate will help to avoid problems of matching work loads with experience and skill levels.

Ministry Titles

It has been said, If you can't give a person a raise, give them a fancy title. This must be true because the role of associate pastor has a wide variety of ministry titles attached to it. With the large number of titles comes confusion about the role and the expectations of the associate pastor from the church as a whole. Some position titles, such as youth director (or youth minister or youth pastor) seem clear enough. An associate with that title should "work with the youth" and attend to any other duties that may be consistent with youth ministry. This broader definition might include serving the families of youth, and any activities that are designed for youth or their families. But, it is usually not that simple. Lawson and Choun reported that thirty-three different position titles were given by 146 members of the Professional Association of Christian Educators (PACE).[2] This does not reflect those associates in the local church whose primary function is not Christian education. It is likely that the total number of titles for associate pastors is much higher.

In a study of current and former educational-ministry staff of ten denominations, Kevin E. Lawson found that "the most outstanding observation is that most educational ministry staff have several areas of responsibility, not just one area." These other areas included occasional preaching, small groups, visitation, and counseling.[3] Titles for associates are being formed around very nontraditional descriptions of ministry, such as Minister of Involvement.[4]

To understand better how the ministry description is formed, it is necessary to discuss what is implied in the title, Director. Are there different expectations for a youth director rather than for a youth minister? How does the role change if the person is called a youth pastor? Is a youth pastor someone who is ordained or licensed, or is the title, Pastor, limited to those who are ordained? Can the title, Youth Pastor, be given to someone who is neither licensed or ordained? Should congregations reserve the title of pastor for the associate who is licensed or ordained? Should all pastoral staff called to serve a church be ordained or licensed? When a person is licensed by the church, should he be called pastor or minister? Is the title, Director, reserved for those who are neither licensed or ordained? What difference does it make what the title of the position is or what the associate is called? As much as we would like to think it should make no difference what the title is, in practice, it does affect the congregation's perception of the associate pastor's role.

The title, Associate Pastor, does not have the advantage of obvious clarity as do the titles, Youth Pastor or Director of Children's Ministries. What does the associate pastor do? It is obvious that this person does not pastor associates, but it is not clear from this position title what is expected by the church. Does the associate pastor do everything that the senior pastor does? Is it clear to everyone why it is necessary for two to fill the post of pastor? What does a director of Christian education direct? How are these more general titles different from those related to an age group? Persons with general titles or combination titles (Music and Youth, or Christian Education and Youth) have more of a problem with role expectations than does the age-group minister. Obviously, churches need to negotiate wisely and delineate clearly, both for themselves and for the associate, what the position title means; then they should clearly communicate the details to the congregation.

If a congregation has had no experience having an associate before, it should be clearly spelled out what the title will be and what the title means for the associate. If a person is called a pastor, then will certain sacerdotal functions be required when necessary? Can the associate, or should the associate, be expected to counsel the hurting; officiate at weddings, funerals, baptisms, communion services, parent and baby dedications; or preach in the senior pastor's absence? If so, is it necessary that the associate be ordained or licensed? Each church will need to answer these questions for themselves so that the expectations for the role of associate are clearer to the congregation.

Ordained, Licensed, or Not

One of my full-time church positions had the title, Director of Christian Education (DCE). No sacerdotal functions such as weddings, baptisms, communion services, or parent and baby dedications were expected of the DCE. Preaching was done rarely but not in the pastor's absence and only in relation to a Christian education emphasis in the worship services. In short, no functions normally carried out by a pastor, either in the church as a whole or with the youth, were done by the DCE. I was not ordained or licensed; I was full-time but thought of as the church's "leading layman."

In another church, I served as an ordained associate. The ordination took place at the conclusion of four and one half years of service in a church as a director. In the new church, all the sacerdotal functions were expected and the title changed to Minister of Christian Education and Youth (MCEY). As an ordained minister, my first funeral, wedding, and communion services were performed in the new setting. When the pastor resigned (fourteen weeks after my arrival), leaving me as the only pastoral staff member, I found that I was expected to carry out all the sacerdotal duties, including preaching, until an interim pastor could be arranged for. My perceptions of my roles as DCE and MCEY had to change because both my title and the expectations that went with it certainly had.

If the sacerdotal functions are *not* required of the associate position, then is it even necessary to seek a person who is ordained? Would a person who is qualified to be licensed be fully acceptable for the associate position? Some churches say no to the associate's ordination and licensing because these churches do not allow for more than one person to serve as pastor. Others appreciate having multiple ordained pastors on staff in various associate roles. They like the variety of choice when they seek someone to assist them with a personal service (such as counseling for a personal problem, or to perform a wedding or a funeral). Parishioners may prefer to have other respected ministers on the staff to whom they can turn.

For those churches who never accepted the idea of having more than one person who serves as their pastor, others on the church staff may be simply considered the senior pastor's assistants. These assistants help in various ways so that the pastor is free to devote himself more completely to specific parts of his work. In this type of church, the congregation would not consider asking any associate for personal help of a spiritual nature because only the senior pastor is satisfactory in such a crisis. The one and only person who serves as pastor is the holy man, and only he will do for spiritual emergencies. Any attempt on the part of the unordained associate to assist in spiritual matters would not be adequate. This leads us to consider whether the associate is a specialist or a generalist.

Specialist or Generalist

No matter what the church polity may be, the view of the church about the associate can take at least two different views. The associate can be a generalist who assists the senior pastor in carrying out any of the tasks of shepherd, evangelist, teacher, or prophet. The generalist is expected to fill in where there is an overload on the senior pastor. The rationale for the calling of an associate under the generalist definition is found in a phrase that is in many associate job descriptions: "to serve as the pastor may direct." This phrase serves as a contingency for a growing congregation and the perception of the pastor that he is unable to keep up with increasing demands on his time.

The specialist approach to the associate role is usually instituted because a pastor feels overloaded, or delegates an entire area or areas of ministry to someone else. This someone else might be a lay person at first, but eventually the responsibilities can grow to a full-time ministry. These areas might be those mentioned in Scripture (shepherd, resident evangelist, the prophet who forth-tells, teaching the Bible), or they may be a specific portion of ministry, such as youth work, children's work, Sunday school, discipleship, small groups, visitation, music, and so forth.

An associate pastor is more likely to be perceived by the congregation as an equal of the senior pastor if the associate is a generalist. Generalists are more often called pastor or minister, and if they are ordained, they carry out sacerdotal functions (those usually fulfilled by clergy) more frequently than specialists do. Generalists more often move to senior-pastor positions than do specialists, and, conversely, specialists tend more often to be career associate pastors than do generalists. Since Scripture doesn't specify an associate's duties, it is up to church leaders to interpret the pastoral role in a way appropriate to their tradition and specific need. Some pastors and churches may prefer a generalist, others a specialist, and the description of the ministry position should reflect that.

Hidden Agendas

Some people in the church may have a set of expectations for the associate that has nothing to do with the written ministry description. These self-appointed activists have a personal agenda that they hope the associate will complete. One of my position titles was Minister of Christian Education and Youth. Soon, I realized some people were far more interested in my reaching the youth who had drifted away from the church than anything else I might do in Christian education. They had youth in their homes or families who, although raised in the church, had little interest in the things of God and were acting out their rebellion. In a way, I was viewed as the messiah and savior of these wayward youth. The youth part of my title was mentioned second, but it had first priority for many (if not most) in the church. There was nothing in writing about the priority of youth in my ministry description. I found that I was evaluated by expectations that were both personally motivated and unwritten.

Associate pastors often find out they are being evaluated from a hidden agenda when they see the annual budget. In none of the full- or part-time associate positions I held over a period of nineteen years did anyone ever ask me how we were existing on the salary the church paid me. I frequently found out that there was a salary raise for the staff by seeing the number published in the annual budget. Each year in one of the churches we served, a budget was presented for approval by the congregation. Right or wrong, I interpreted the budget like this: a modest increase implied that I had done okay during the previous year and that the church had given me a passing grade at evaluation time. A big increase meant they were thrilled with my service and wanted to reward me. A salary cut would normally be the result of severe shortfalls in church income, but when church income was there, a salary freeze or cut would imply that I had been found wanting. At one church's annual meeting, I discovered that the budget figure for my salary was frozen at the same amount as the year before. Inflation was running annually in the double digits at the time, so the salary freeze was really a cut. I felt devastated, not because I had received an unfavorable evaluation but because there were no explanations of exactly where I had fallen short. The hidden expectations had struck me with great force.

Personality Fit

It is also possible that the hidden expectations for the associate may be related to the type of personality sought for that position. It could be that an associate will be sought who is in some way an extension of the senior pastor. Some senior pastors want the associate to be clones of themselves in order to validate their style of ministry. For instance, if an assertive and dominant (a high D on the DiSC™ Profile) senior pastor needs an associate, what may be sought is not a retiring and submissive (a high C or S) associate. The search may be for someone who is also assertive and dominant. The high D associate would find it easy to fulfill the expectations of the senior pastor because of similar characteristics. The high C or S associate would be intimidated and would be found wanting if even called to serve there in the first place.

Others realize their own weaknesses of personality and draw around them associates who complement them. For example, if a senior pastor is a high C with the gift of administration, then he may seek an associate who is a high I with the gift of teaching or exhortation. A senior pastor who is a high D or I and also an evangelist can help the church by bringing an educator and administrator on staff. The pastor who is a visionary will need an organizer to help fulfill those visions. Building a team of staff members who complements one another helps to develop a more complete ministry. All the spiritual gifts are given to build up the body of Christ, and the church staff should be examined to see if personality types and spiritual gifts are being utilized in the most effective way. The senior pastor who recognizes his own strengths and shortcomings can complement his own qualities by wise staff selection. While this sounds fine, there is at least one reason why it does not always work out.

Some senior pastors will not approve the call of another to share in their ministry if he finds it difficult working with an associate who is more skilled than he in some aspect of ministry. If the senior pastor is an excellent administrator, and the associate an excellent evangelist, can the senior pastor handle the increased visibility and attention given to the associate by the church? Can the senior pastor listen to the associate's ministry being praised without being personally threatened? We will talk about this more later, but these dynamics do affect the expectations of the associate either before the call occurs or after the associate arrives on the scene.

Conclusion

The role expectations of the church are not irrelevant to the effectiveness or perceived effectiveness of the associate pastor. Role expectation is affected by the type of covenant the church uses. The associate's ministry description affects the ways in which its fulfillment is measured. To most church members, the sad fact is that the title, Associate Pastor, is not well understood. To be associated with the pastor does not necessarily mean that anything is shared related to authority or responsibility. To the congregation as a whole, ministerial titles may have little meaning, and the meaning and process of ordination may be unfamiliar. For those on the church staff, these issues are very important, but the sad fact is that congregants will likely have little interest. The next chapter will focus on examining role expectations from the perspective of the associate.

Discussion Questions

Use these questions privately or in a group, such as a church staff, to apply the points made in this chapter.

1. Does your actual (unwritten) church covenant match your official (written) one? If no, in what way(s) does it differ?

2. Find the written ministry description for each associate on the church staff. (If there is none, create one that fits your situation.) Note the main categories of duties and determine if those duties are detailed and exact, or if they are vague and general.

3. Is there a history in your church that accounts for the associate's ministry description being written the way it is (vague or specific)?

4. Are the expectations of the church in line with the type of ministry description it is? (A vague description that has vague expectations?)

5. Are there hidden or unwritten expectations by the congregation that are not written on the ministry description? How would you find out?

6. Are the duties expected of the associate appropriate to the amount of time expected to fulfill them? Are a certain number of hours specified in the written ministry description?

7. Does the title of the associate clearly reflect the duties that are expected to be filled?

8. If the terms *minister* or *pastor* are used in the title of an associate, are sacerdotal expectations in the ministry description?

9. Is the pastoral staff of your church organized as generalists, specialists, or a combination of both? What advantages does your configuration have for your church? What disadvantages can you observe from your current title? Would changing the arrangement from generalist to specialist or vice versa increase efficiency and/or a sense of fulfillment by the associates?

10. Does the church as a whole expect that there is more than one holy man in the congregation to whom they could go with their spiritual concerns?

11. Are all associates on a church staff treated equally in regard to title and expectations of service? Do all the associates understand completely the ministry responsibilities of each other? If not, why not?

12. Do the talents and gifts of the associate match the ministry description for that associate?

13. Are there allowances made for the career growth of the associate in the ministry description? Explain.

14. Are there allowances made for changes in the staff configuration (number and specific duties)?

15. What evidence can you produce that reveals the level of integrity on the part of the associate's pastoral supervisor(s)? What about the integrity level of the associate?

16. Under what criteria is the fulfillment of the ministry description to be evaluated or judged satisfactory? Is any evaluation item included in the ministry description?

17. Does the associate's ministry description fit into an integrated and complementary pattern of staff service for the whole church?

18. Is there any area of the associate's ministry description that causes a personal threat to the senior pastor or any other associate? Is there any duty that might cause a personal threat to anyone?

CHAPTER FIVE

How Do I Want to Play This Part?
(Expectations of the Associate)

Every associate should determine how they are going to perform the part assigned to them in the pastoral ensemble. The associate needs to know if he or she has expectations about performance that will possibly interfere with what the church expects. Any such interferences will definitely create wrong notes and bad sounding music. What are typical expectations that associates bring into the pastoral ensemble? How would the church know what those expectations were?

Aspirations

One of the times when I served on a pastoral search committee, I was one of two representatives from the elder board. We examined scores of résumés (they numbered about seventy) from potential candidates, some of whom lived nearby and others who were from out of state. Some were associates hoping to move to a senior-pastor position and others were senior or solo pastors hoping to move into another place of service. Some were students about to graduate and looking for a first position after graduation. Some were working in ministries other than the pastorate and wanted us to consider them for our pastor. Some were not in ministry at all, but wanted to either enter it for the first time or reenter it. From the large response, it was obvious that the competition for the position was intense.

I am sure that many of the candidates were shocked to learn that they could not be considered for the pastorate of our church for one reason or another. After all, there was only one position available. The dreams of the candidates crashed into reality, and many who wanted a senior or solo pastorate realized that to be in the ministry at all, they would need to consider being an associate.

The possibility of being an associate may come as a shock to the pastor-to-be because many have never aspired to be an associate.

This is particularly true for those who come to the end of their seminary careers and begin looking for a church position. Many of these pastoral candidates will be forced to take an associate position because churches pass them by for other, more experienced senior-pastor candidates. Perhaps they were not prepared for the fact that the competition was so fierce. The high number of vacant churches may not be of the type or in the location that the candidate was seeking. The goal of some graduates to become solo or senior pastors was not reached as they had envisioned. They found they would have to "settle" for being an associate or choose to support themselves in some activity that was not vocational ministry. Associates who enter the ministry in this manner often experience conflicts with their own role expectations.

Associates who are aspiring senior pastors may have a constant struggle with the desire to fulfill functions reserved traditionally for the senior minister. In some cases, they possess an educational background that is equal to or greater than that of the senior pastor. If the senior pastor has a master of divinity degree and the associate pastor presents a résumé with the same degree, confusion can arise as the associate realizes that his ministerial preparation was to carry out activities assigned to the senior pastor. The job description of the associate position may not match the focus of the associate's educational preparation. This may be a big surprise to the associate. The mind-set of these associates must be adjusted to this unexpected situation.

Throughout their seminary training, these individuals may have concentrated most of their study and internship experiences toward becoming a senior (with a multiple staff) or solo (with no other pastoral staff) pastor. There have been dreams of doing senior or solo pastor-type duties such as preaching, comforting the afflicted, and shepherding God's people. Somehow, administering a Sunday school program, running an active youth ministry, and finding people to fill slots in the church nursery does not fit easily into those dreams.

Role Models

A problem may arise if aspiring associates have only observed one (solo) pastor in a church body and have had little or no acquaintance with anyone who ever served in the associate position. They have had few role models to emulate. Even if associates have attended a large, multistaffed church, they may have had no personal acquaintance either personally or professionally with associates serving vocationally on the church staff. Exposure to appropriate role models is very important to the success of aspiring associates.

In some cases, seminaries perpetuate the concept that the associate pastor is second class. In twenty-one years as a Christian college and seminary professor, I have observed that role models invited to Christian college or seminary chapels or classrooms as guest speakers seldom include associate pastors. More frequently, those pastors asked to be guests on campus are senior pastors of large churches with multiple staff associates, and associates seldom accompany the senior pastor to outside speaking engagements. The message is not very subtle; success is being a senior pastor who preaches well and the goal toward which all seminarians should aspire. No wonder seminary students who are pastors-to-be have little concept of what an associate is or does.

Family and Friends

Another source of misunderstanding that affects the associate's role expectations can come from those closest to us. Our families and friends, of course, are subject to misunderstandings regarding the role of pastoral leadership. Why should friends and family be exempt from attitudes that confuse the associate role? It hurts to hear family or friends express confusion about why one would want to be an associate pastor. Family gatherings can take on a negative cast and may even be avoided so as to eliminate the questions about your next vocational move. Questions about when you will "grow up" and take a church of "your own" become less than amusing when repeated. Perhaps they mean to ask, When will the associate become a professional?

Professionalism

The issue of professionalism has had an interesting application to the role expectations of pastors and pastoral associates. Langham has schematized the criteria for professionalism in science as "(1) rigorous training by competent practitioners of the discipline, (2) earning a living based on one's contributions to the subject, (3) the propagation of one's scientific contributions by training students who will earn their living from the subject, (4) the utilization or establishment of whatever institutions are necessary to fulfill the second and third criteria, and (5) the production of scientific contributions that are sufficiently technical as to be understandable only to a group of fellow practitioners which therefore functions as the exclusive judge and audience for one's work." [1]

The criteria for professionalism in science may not exactly fit the ministry, but note the parallels between them. (1) Rigorous training should be a part of the associate's background. Even the scientists do not specify which degrees are required for specific fields, only that training be rigorous. Should the associate's training be anything less?

(2) Earning a living through your practice is also rather vague because someone who gets paid for his ministerial service may or may not fulfill any of the other criteria. Making a living from the ministry does imply that others have recognized your skills and are willing to allow you the freedom to exercise your gifts among them. This criteria validates the associate position from another source.

(3) Training students to carry on the ministry is central to the disciple-making ministry of the associate. Spiritually reproducing oneself should be at the heart of the associate's (or any minister's) work. The training of students in ministry may not be as formal as implied by the scientists, but the product should be the same. (4) The creation of institutions to carry out the training has already been accomplished in and through the local or parachurch. Not much more needs to be done to meet this criteria. (5) Producing information understandable to only those within the scientific community seems, at first glance, to be unrelated to ministry. There is a sense in which the propagation of the content of ministry should be distributed as widely as possible, to help as many people as possible become a part of the work of ministry. To restrict the content of ministry only to those engaged in it would violate the very purpose of making disciples. There is a sense, however, of appropriate restriction of the content of ministry. Are there not certain elements of ministry that only a person involved in it would understand? Are there not some aspects of ministry that would be appropriately restricted to ministerial practitioners?

For our purposes, the term *professional* will signify those in ministry who possess specialized training for the work of ministry, with standards for admission and expulsion set by practitioners. The minister's skills will be recognized by the Christian community, and people will be edified by his ministry. Early in this country's history, there were few professions, but today, nearly everyone from hairdressers to taxi-cab drivers refers to his or her work as a profession. So how is the associate pastor a professional?

Many believe that the associate pastor is best viewed as a professional in the same sense that the senior pastor is a professional. In this paradigm, the roles and functions of each must be clearly differentiated, but both senior and associate should be viewed as serving in the profession of ministry. There are certain bodies of specialized knowledge that would qualify the ministry as a profession, but some would question the self-regulating aspects of the ministry. Some denominations fulfill the regulatory function, but most independent and nonaffiliated congregations have little regulation. Without regulation, can the ministry be considered a profession? Is an associate pastor a professional? It may be popular to think of the associate position as professional, but the lack of regulation raises a legitimate question of whether or not it is professional. Perhaps the associate is a functionary.

The term *functionary* is used to distinguish certain roles that are repetitive and routine in nature. A functionary's tasks may be mundane or elaborately complex, but they are duties that carry out the policies determined by the employer. A functionary is thought of not as a person who is looked to for original thought or plans but as one who completes tasks with little regard for how any policy suits specific people or situations. Is the associate pastor primarily a functionary? The routine and repetitive nature of some aspects of ministry will no doubt be present in most, if not all, ministries, but it does not seem that the functionary is an appropriate model for the associate pastor.

Another term that might be applied to the associate is *amateur*. This word comes from the Latin word for love, and when referring to work, is thought to mean "to do the work for the love of it." One is thought to be an amateur if one works or plays without compensation. The connotation for *amateur* carries a high level of motivation and commitment that is derived from the work itself. The work itself is reward enough, as in a person's hobby. This status of amateur does not necessarily reflect a poor quality of performance, for some amateurs exhibit a very high level of skill. Some amateurs are the best in the world at what they do. A common application of this term had been to Olympic athletes, that is before performance fees or compensation for endorsements were allowed. Is the associate pastor better thought of as an amateur?

The mind-set of the amateur—high motivation and enthusiasm in the work of ministry—can also be an excellent framework for the expectations of the associate pastor, senior pastor, or layperson. The associate who is free from greedily seeking after salary raises, benefits, or perks is free to devote much more energy to the tasks of ministry. Such a person might be bivocational. Church boards would be delighted to find pastors who serve as a team and also function in their roles as amateurs. Church budgets could allocate less to staff salaries and those monies could be directed elsewhere. However, if associates are viewed as professionals, it is important that salaries be commensurate with their education, skills, and responsibilities. More about salary and benefits will be discussed in the next chapter.

Career or Job

The concept of career is one more point to keep in mind before associates decide what roles they should expect of themselves. A career is a specific type of task one does for a period of life. This does not mean that a person will be employed in one particular career for his or her whole life, because the average person in America changes careers four or five times. Changing a certain job does not require changing the career. One could speak of a career in the ministry and have worked in a great variety of Christian organizations. Thus, though associates serve in various churches and wear varied titles, they can still be considered to have a ministerial career as an associate pastor.

In my opinion, the best perspective for associate pastors encompasses a combination of the professional and amateur models in a lifelong church-based career. The element of professionalism that is helpful is the self-regulation through accountability that ministers impose on themselves to live a godly life before the people. The best kind of regulation comes from within as each person lives a life of integrity before God. There are also ways the associate can have regulation from the outside, such as through the official board of the church. The amateur elements are the passionate drive to serve God and the freedom from worldly inducements that reward that service. To serve God is its own reward. The functionary element of the unfeeling fulfillment of mechanical duties should be overcome by compassionate caring of the people being served by the associate. It is helpful to understand that the career associate role can be a lifelong commitment and still be fulfilling and totally within the will of God for that person.

To Be Mentored

One of the expectations that many associates have is personal. Many associates have confided to me that they were appalled to learn that their senior pastor had little interest in being a spiritual mentor. They wanted to work with a certain pastor with the hope that they would become personally and closely related to him through vulnerability and intimacy, and they have concluded that this will not happen. They ask if they were naive or if their expectation was wrong.

Many associates expect to be held accountable for the fulfillment of the tasks that are assigned to them. Many associates also expect to be held accountable for personal, spiritual issues. There is an expectation by the associate that the senior pastor display vulnerability with the associate. Instead of a warm, caring, and supportive relationship, the associate finds accountability limited to duties and responsibilities that are listed in the ministry description or assigned by the pastor. When the associate shares deeply about intimate details, and the senior pastor does not reciprocate, the associate is left stranded emotionally. A conflict arises when the senior wants primarily a business relationship and the associate wants primarily a personal one. The disparity causes disillusionment on the part of both.

Depending on the background of the associate, there may be a great need for the support sought from the senior pastor. If there is abuse or other types of dysfunctionality in the associate's past life, the senior pastor may be sought after to help heal those hurts. If the associate is relatively mature in an emotional and spiritual sense, then the associate's expectation might not be as great for the senior pastor to fill a role as counselor. The difference in age and in experience in ministry between the associate and the senior pastor could play a major role in establishing expectations.

Education

One other element that affects the expectations of the associate is ministerial education. While some larger churches are beginning pastoral training programs themselves, the majority still desire some formal training for Christian ministry. One job description seen recently for a Christian education director states that Christian lifestyle, maturity, experience, and character will be viewed more significantly than formal training. The lack of reference to any required formal training may indicate that the position level being sought is for a nonprofessional, nonordained, lay person. Theological training is still sought by most churches for ministerial candidates, but since the establishment of Bible institutes or colleges, and now Christian colleges and universities, the matter of theological education has become a bit more complex.

When a person graduates from a Bible institute or Bible college, to what extent have they experienced training for a life of ministry? Some denominations have no seminaries (Foursquare and Open Bible) and the Bible college (L.I.F.E. in Los Angeles, California, and Eugene Bible College in Oregon) serves to train ministerial candidates. In the case where denominations have their own seminaries, the educational standard for candidates in that group usually requires a seminary degree. Nondenominational churches waiver regarding educational requirements for associates, depending on a number of factors. There is little uniformity among the churches of America regarding educational requirements for associate pastors. Such requirements can vary from none beyond high school to an advanced degree beyond seminary training.

Those who do graduate from a Bible institute or Bible college may have differing expectations for service than does a nongraduate. The seminary graduate will certainly have differing expectations from a nonseminary graduate. Will a seminary graduate expect to do more and be given more responsibility than someone with less education? Will students who graduate from Bible college and serve for a few years raise their expectations when they graduate from seminary? What affect does one's education (the length, type, and extent) have on what one may be asked to do?

Degrees

Consider those with a doctor of ministry (D.Min.), a doctor of philosophy (Ph.D.), or a doctor of education (Ed.D.) degree who want to serve as associate pastors. That an associate has a higher educational degree than the senior pastor would be enough for some senior pastors to refuse such a candidate an interview. Kevin Lawson, in his 1994 study, found that over half of the current and former educational staff members have a graduate-level education, with the master's degree being most prevalent, at 34 percent. (Interestingly, the bachelor's degree was next most prevalent, with 30.1 percent.) The M.Div. was 15.2 percent, and any type of doctorate totaled 7.8 percent.[2] Why do so few associates have doctoral degrees?

One reason could be that the threat of their having one may be too much for the senior pastor to bear. Many other excuses besides the doctorate may conveniently be used as the reason that a candidate is unsuitable. If pastoral egos are weak, associates with doctoral degrees may find themselves forced out of the market for most church staff positions. They may be viewed as overqualified. Even those senior pastors with doctoral degrees may feel threatened if their egos will not allow anyone else on staff who has a similar level of education. Threats to the pastoral ego are not usually the kind of things that an associate would think about when discussing expectations for a new job, but those threats do exist. Senior pastors and associate candidates should be ready for this kind of discussion.

Conclusion

Throughout the candidating process the associate must seek clarity in regard to what specific role he or she will be expected to fill in the prospective church. The candidate should not avoid asking pointed questions during the interviews. A level of agreement must be sought, even though agreement on the part of all may be hard to achieve. Certainly the senior pastor and official church board should be aware of these distinctions and which particular definition or combination of definitions will serve as their operational definition for the associate pastor.

Are there such persons out there to fill the associate pastor role? Do they still exist? Yes, there are those who feel called to associate pastoral roles and are well suited to function in these capacities. These are men and women who feel called to serve the Lord Jesus Christ in his church as associates and have no desire to move to other roles. They do not yield to pressure from others or from within to change roles because they enjoy immensely serving in the local church in ways that best fit their spiritual gifts, natural abilities, and talents.

Paul in his letter to Ephesus prayed that God "who is able to do immeasurably more than we ask or imagine, according to his power that is at work within us, to him be glory in the church and in Christ Jesus throughout all generations, for ever and ever! Amen" (3:20–21). Any of our expectations should be lifted up to God and given to him. It is he who will carry out his will in us and exceed all that we might expect. When our expectations are given over to him, we have nothing to fear and everything to anticipate.

Any expectations of the associate will affect greatly how the assigned functions are fulfilled. In the next part of this book, we will examine some key relationships in the associate pastor's life, beginning with the most crucial.

Discussion Questions

Use these questions privately or in a group, such as a church staff, to apply the points made in this chapter.

1. Do the expectations of the associate(s) in your church closely match the church's ministry position(s)?

2. Do the associate ministers in your church view their ministry as a life-long calling or do they expect to move into a senior-pastor position sometime in the future?

3. How has the answer to question two affected their current ministry? How might it affect their ministry in the future?

4. Do the associates on your staff view themselves as professionals, functionaries, amateurs, a combination of the three, or something else? What makes you answer the way you did?

5. What adjustments (from question four) would help the associate's expectations match those of the church?

6. How does the level of education possessed by members of the church staff affect their expectations regarding their ministry functions?

7. Do any of the associates have the same or a higher educational degree than the senior pastor? How has this situation been handled?

8. Does the associate expect to be treated as equal with the senior pastor? On what is your answer based?

9. Can you verify the existence of threats to senior members of the church staff by junior members? If so, how?

10. How can any threat within the staff be resolved or neutralized?

11. Is there a desire on the part of the associates for a mentoring-type relationship from the senior pastor? Is there a difference between the expected and the reality? Why?

12. Should an associate expect to be involved in a personal mentoring relationship with the senior pastor? Why or why not?

Part 3:
Relationships

CHAPTER SIX

How Should I Play with the First-Chair Player?
(The Senior Pastor)

The first chair of each instrument in the orchestra is occupied by the best performer for that instrument. In the violin section, the first chair is also designated the concertmaster or concertmistress. In addition to playing the first part or lead, and any solos that may be called for, this person serves to moderate any business meetings, conducts tuning of the instruments before rehearsals or concerts, and, in general, acts as the president of the orchestra. In many ways, the senior pastor is the first-chair player in the pastoral orchestra. The associates relationship with the senior pastor is very important for the creation of beautiful music.

Some senior pastors wish that a verse from Psalm 23 (with some adaptation) were true when it comes to the church staff. They would like verse 4 to read, "My staff they comfort me." While this may be true in some cases, the research on the matter reveals another point of view. When associate pastors get together their complaints focus on staff relationships and specifically the relationship with the senior pastor. Kevin Lawson's study revealed that educational ministry staff have consistently reported that one of their struggles in ministry has been the stress, communication difficulties, and conflict with their pastoral supervisors. His findings have confirmed the earlier studies by Tharp (1976), and by Hipps and Helms (1981), which have concluded the same thing.[1] Moving on seems easier than staying and dealing with the conflicts.

During the candidating period at one of the churches I served, I asked the pastor, who had been there twenty years, if he had any plans for leaving the church. "After all," I said, "twenty years is a long time." He told me, "We never know how God is going to lead us." I should have recognized a warning flag when he said that, but instead I made an almost fatal assumption. Instead of telling me a strong "no" and that he was committed to working with me for some time to come, he waffled and implied he was not sure. I should have followed up on his statement because soon (about fourteen weeks later) after I moved my family 2,500 miles and came to work with him, he resigned. It became increasingly obvious to me that he had planned all along to leave and was just waiting for an associate to come so he could step out gracefully. There is more to this story, but at that point I came closer to leaving the ministry, as a result of his leaving, than at any time in my life. The relationship I thought we could enjoy never had a chance to develop. It was over soon after it started.

Some of the things I have heard from associates include "My senior pastor knows little about my specific job, yet he insists on telling me how to do it"; "My pastor is only concerned about obedience, particularly my obeying his instructions. He treats me like a child with no mind of my own"; "I wish I could talk openly with my senior pastor on a personal basis and let ministry business wait. I know that if I am transparent with what I am really feeling about my ministry, I run the risk of losing my job because he would use it against me." These are a few of the things some associates say about the problem that looms largest before them.

There is no more important single human relationship for the effectiveness of the associate pastor than his relationship with the senior pastor. That is not to say the relationship with the Lord Jesus Christ is not an important relationship, for it is, of course. How can one serve the Lord Jesus effectively and tenaciously without a growing, personal relationship with Him? An associate might think he or she is rightly related to Jesus and still be badly related to the senior pastor. If that is true, the associate will soon find that there is no future in continued service at that church. Notice I said there is no more important single "human relationship," which takes care of the relationship with Jesus Christ, but what about the spouse, if there is one?

The spouse, if the associate happens to be married, is also important and frequently provides the encouragement and support that is necessary for perseverance in ministry during the hard times. But the effectiveness of the associate in ministry responsibilities is not usually directly dependent on his or her spouse, as important as that support may be. The spouse is important, but not as important as the relationship to the senior pastor when it comes to professional effectiveness. What then should be the vital ingredients of the relationship with the senior pastor?

Integrity

The most notable single factor to assess in the relationship with the senior pastor is personal integrity. The concept of integrity is difficult to describe, but has been defined as honesty or character.

The Bible is replete with examples of men and women of both excellent and not so excellent character. David, for example, was "a man after God's own heart." True, he sinned, but because he recognized his sin, grieved over it, and asked for forgiveness (see Ps. 51). He was a man of character because he agreed with God about his sin and was not afraid to own his sin. David was honest, a man of his word, and sensitive to God's direction in his life.

How can integrity be assessed in someone else or even yourself? Integrity as a character quality is difficult to measure or even observe in the short period of time given to most candidating interviews. Most candidating experiences consist of churches scheduling a "blitz" of meetings, with various groups asking and answering questions all on one weekend. The vote to call the person is often made the Sunday night of the same weekend. Integrity is easily assumed when there is insufficient time to observe it. The associate may reason, After all, the man is the senior pastor of the church. Being in that position, he must be a man of integrity. Such a rush to vote on calling the associate often backfires. Only later does the wisdom of taking more time to get to know each other surface.

Authority and Power

Integrity is a complex issue, but power and authority will be a significant part of the working environment. The issue of power and authority will always be present in a church-staff relationship because power and authority exist in human relationships. Although power is defined as the general ability to produce a certain occurrence, it implies the force, if necessary, to control or command others.[2] Authority is the degree of influence people ascribe to others. That influence may be earned or unearned.[3] Gardner sees authority as legitimized power, i.e., a mandate to exercise power in a certain sphere.[4] Habecker explains by saying, "If I have power, I have the ability to control; but if the power I have has not been authorized, the power I exercise becomes suspect. Further, even though might does not make right, there cannot be any authority without power."[5] Pastors usually possess the authority of the office they hold. Others have authority ascribed to them because the local church body perceives a high level of commitment of the pastoral-staff member to the body. There may have been a stalwart response by the pastor to a crisis in the church or in personal lives that caused him to be viewed as authoritative.

Most associates know where the power and authority lie in the church. A pastor with whom I worked for many years told me, "If two men ride a horse, one must be in front!" I understood him to mean that he was in front and that I was in the back. I also thought he was saying that I should be content with riding behind him. Jesus spoke of servanthood and there has been much written about that subject. Unfortunately, very little speaks about the power and authority issues among the church staff.[6] Let me tell you about an experience that demonstrates what I mean about authority on a church staff.

One meeting of the Christian education committee that I was attending early on in my ministry was held in the pastor's study. The room was not really a study for there were no books, files, or other tools for study. The room was bare except for a large desk with a large high-back chair behind it that dominated the room. Smaller and less comfortable chairs were positioned around the perimeter of the room with seating for twelve to fifteen. There was a door to the secretary's office and a private entrance to the outside. The pastor's study had a private rest room located behind and to one side of the desk. The chairman of the committee sat on a chair next to the front edge of the desk so he could place his notes on it. The rest of us were seated around the perimeter of the room in no particular order. The senior pastor sat in the high-backed chair behind his desk. I was the new minister of education and had only been in the church about two weeks. I barely knew the names of the committee members, but I recognized authority when I saw it.

The chairman led the meeting by opening with prayer and proceeded by raising questions and topics from a list he had in front of him. There was no written agenda for the rest of us; we had to guess what was coming next. One item I especially remember was deciding on the quantity of supplies to purchase and, specifically, how many boxes of paper clips should be ordered for the teacher's supply cabinet. After each question on the chairman's agenda, various committee members spoke up, giving opinions. When everyone who wished to do so had a chance to talk, the chairman usually asked the pastor for his opinion. When the pastor had given his opinion, a vote was taken. In every case, as I recall, the vote of the committee was supportive of the pastor's opinion. The senior pastor's authority (and also power) was very clear to me. I began to wonder how I was going to function in this new situation.

Before the meeting adjourned, I asked if they would allow me to stock the teacher's supply cabinet without prior approval, and they gratefully said yes. I also asked if they would allow me to shape the agenda for our meetings in cooperation with the pastor and the chairman of the committee, and then send it to them by mail at least one week in advance of our monthly meeting. I wanted to do this so they could more carefully consider and pray about the best way to resolve the issues. They also agreed to that. I thought I had made a little progress.

The meetings that followed were very similar in structure in that the pastor's approval of any item was requested by the chairman of the committee before the committee voted to approve. The difference was that each of the items on the agenda had now been previously approved by the pastor in our weekly staff meetings. I would not place anything on the agenda for which I did not have prior approval from the pastor. That meant that there were some very vigorous discussions in some of our staff meetings. Some of my ideas were modified and some dropped altogether, but when we went to the committee, we went as a united team. It was a novel concept to the committee for they were accustomed to disagreements and arguments between the senior pastor and other staff members. They still depended on the senior pastor for guidance, but having a united front from the staff was thought by them to be real progress.

The authority of the pastor was not compromised; he still had veto power over any and all ideas. What I gained was access to approval for my ideas. I don't believe any manipulation was involved in this procedure because nothing was concealed from the pastor. In fact, more open communication occurred than had ever before, according to his own report. A wise associate knows where the authority lies and works with it to achieve goals that he or she has in mind. Now what about communication on a personal level with the senior pastor?

Communication

Most associates find it difficult to share anything from their personal lives with the senior pastor with whom they work. Any frustration or lack of skill is closely guarded and restricted from the knowledge of the pastor. One reason for limiting openness is because any personal deficiency can be viewed as a weakness and possible cause for dismissal. For these reasons, associates are usually very careful about sharing anything personal that places them in a position of weakness.

If I were to share something personal with my pastor (and let's not forget that the senior pastor is the associate's pastor), how would it be received? The tension between the associate's needing to share the frustration that is paralyzing action and the risk of appearing incompetent is a very real one. Unless the associate can get over the fear of sharing openly and deeply with the pastor, there will be little open communication. More than one associate has resigned because he or she said the wrong thing or, because of paralyzing fear, said nothing.

It would be wonderful if the senior pastor took the lead in the relationship and modeled a transparent and open partnership. The associate would therefore be more at ease doing the same. There is the risk, of course, that the senior pastor will be viewed by the associate as weak and unworthy of trust: how can someone who is so needy be a spiritual leader of the church? It is this very fear that causes many senior pastors to refuse to take the lead in this area. It is this fear of being viewed as inadequate that compels many pastors to act in phony and plastic ways with the associate staff. The hypocritical façade hides the pain behind the mask known by both but acknowledged by neither.

If the associate desires and needs an open and transparent relationship with the senior pastor, it is usually the associate who must initiate that kind of relationship. This does not mean the senior pastor does not desire it or would not find it helpful also, but the position the senior pastor holds in the church tends to mitigate against open and transparent relationships. How many pastors experience quality relationships with anyone? As mentioned earlier, David Smith, in his book, claims that deep friendships, wherein anything can be said without fear of destroying the friendship, are rare among American men.[7] Becoming a senior or associate pastor changes little about how transparent we are with others.

In fact, the authoritative role of senior pastor tends to support the view that there is no one to whom he can go and share what is on his heart. Pastors often think, *To share my weaknesses with any member of my congregation would be disaster. The same would be true of a colleague in another church. There is no one I can trust within the congregation and certainly not a staff member. They could use something I said against me when a showdown occurs. No, I dare not reveal my real self to anyone in or outside my church.* This attitude is unfortunate, especially from the standpoint of the associate. The associate is in need of openness and transparency but often finds no one on the church staff with whom that can occur.

One pastor with whom I worked was known for not being open with anyone in the congregation. This pastor was approaching retirement age, so he announced to the church that he would retire on a certain date, some fourteen months away. This was done to allow sufficient time for the church to find a pastor to replace him. While that action had benefits for pastoral replacement, it had detrimental effects on both of the associate pastors. Any plan for new programs or changes within the existing programs was tabled because the new pastor (whomever he might be) might not approve of it. The effect was to paralyze the associate staff for over a year as far as program development was concerned.

The answer was to develop a plan that would work on another front. The youth minister and his wife, with my wife and I (as minister of education) devised a plan to change the kind of communication within the staff. We decided that since the pastor was retiring, we had nothing to lose by being more open and transparent with him. Why would he fire us knowing he was leaving? Only in the most dire of circumstances (moral failure) would he consider that option. We decided to share our hearts with him and see if that would change his communication with us. We agreed together to try and make the last year of his ministry his best one.

Our plan was to have monthly get-togethers of the staff families, mainly for social reasons. We celebrated birthdays, anniversaries, Groundhog Day, or anything else that served as an excuse to get together. The associates took the initiative to set these up. Also, at the regular weekly staff meetings, each of us rotated the assignment to lead "devotions." When the pastor led, a passage of Scripture was read and a brief and general prayer was offered. When the associates led, we shared more personal struggles and/or specific things from the Word that the Lord was teaching us at the time. Our prayer times took longer, and more personal requests were shared. There was a large difference between our devotions and those of the senior pastor. The monthly social events and the weekly meetings went on for about seven months before there was a change.

At one staff meeting where the senior was scheduled to lead devotions, he invited us into his office. After telling us to close the door and sit down, he shared a personal struggle he was having at that time. Through his tears, he said that no one in the church knew this, and he had told no one but his wife and the Lord. He asked us what he should do. We felt very privileged to be told. We offered counsel and encouragement to him, and we prayed with him about this issue. We felt we had broken through the wall he had built around himself, or more accurately, he broke through his self-imposed wall. It was a significant day in my life to know that when I opened myself, I could do so without fear. We rejoiced that the senior pastor trusted us enough to share with us his innermost self without fear of our breaking confidence and possibly ruining his reputation. It was at that moment I felt an overwhelming love for the man. We had experienced communication on a deep level.

Salary and Benefits

An area where integrity and open communication are primary is in the salary and benefits of the associate. It is not often considered, but the senior pastor plays a pivotal role in the salary of the associate.

When I was called to one church, the pastor told me of the salary when he telephoned to convey the call the church had made to me and my family. The figure was substantially less than I was earning in my then-current position. I later found out that the reason the salary offer was so low was because the senior pastor's salary was unusually low also. He requested that his salary be kept at the low level to help the church budget and to help him avoid paying taxes on income that, in his view, he did not require. This benefited the church, but it did not assist me as an associate to feed my family. The pastor promised to see to it that I received salary increases if I came. We accepted the call, and I found he was a man of his word. We received three salary increases in the first year.

After I had left that position, I was speaking with a member of that church, where I served for five years as an associate pastor, and he brought up the issue of my salary. We had since moved from the area and were no longer attending that church. The friend from our former church mentioned that he was serving on the church finance committee and had occasion to see the figures for salaries from past years. He admitted that he was appalled at the numbers he saw for the staff and especially for my salary. As a regular church member he either did not pay attention to staff salaries or they were not disclosed, but in his new position he found that the figures were, in his opinion, astoundingly low. He asked how I had lived on such a small sum. I did not know what to say, so I mumbled something to the effect that the Lord had provided for us. My friend was, in effect, apologizing on behalf of the church.

I learned through my friend, without my asking, that my successor on the church staff received exactly twice the amount of salary that I had received when I left the church staff. The new person was fulfilling the same role functions I had, but lacked both formal education in Christian education and the number of years of experience I had. My friend told me that the larger salary was due to the senior pastor "going to bat" for the associate. The new senior pastor could not see how anyone could live in the community where the church was located without receiving this higher salary.

In both cases, the senior pastor significantly influenced how the salary of the associate was determined. There is a "staircase effect" at work here that affects the equity issue. No associate will receive the same or more salary as the senior pastor because he is not perceived as having the same level of authority and responsibility as the senior pastor. According to an often unwritten hierarchy, the salaries are spaced apart as stairs on a staircase. If the highest step (as in the first example) is low, the salaries below it will, by necessity, be lower.

Associate salaries are determined by where on the staircase the salaries of all of the staff are and where the top step is located.

Another factor in determining salaries is the degree of willingness on the part of the senior pastor to go to bat for the associates. If the senior pastor feels it is necessary to speak on behalf of the associate before he or she comes to begin work at the church, he may do so because he assumes the associate may not come if the salary is not considered high enough. If the associate has been serving on staff for some time and requests a salary review, the willingness of the senior pastor to speak on behalf of the associate may indicate the level of support the senior has for the associate's ministry and the level of enthusiasm for continuing the relationship. If the senior pastor refuses to speak up for a salary raise for the associate, it could indicate a lack of support for the associate's ministry.

The associate who raises the question of when and how much his next salary raise will be runs some significant risks. The first risk is to discover that the senior pastor does not support the associate after all, at least not enough to tell the official board they need to raise the associate's salary. It may be a difficult circumstance if the associate finds out that the support he or she thought was there is in reality lacking. That lack of support may eventually lead to the departure of the associate with ill feelings toward the pastor and/or the church.

Another risk in asking for a raise is that the associate might be thought of as a money-grubber—a greedy person who does not serve God with a pure motive of sacrifice. This is also a difficult circumstance because it touches to the heart of who the associate is. Can a person of integrity who is serving God with no desire for personal gain ask for a raise and not violate his character? Or is it simply a matter of *appearing* to be greedy that we fear? Or is it acceptable to be greedy if we do not appear so to others who matter to us? These risks are significant enough to have caused me to consider my personal approach to salaries and the money issue.

In the interview for my most recent position as a part-time associate minister of Christian education, I was asked to outline the duties of the position I felt I could fill and that the church needed. When I presented the ministry description, the pastor asked me about compensation. I told him that was a matter between him and the elder board, and that any amount they saw as adequate for the services rendered would be acceptable to me. This had the effect of placing the burden on the board for deciding the compensation. I had the option of rejecting the offer, but I had already said that any amount would be acceptable. I could hardly rescind that and tell them their offer was insufficient. I found their offer to be, on the contrary, very generous. Would I have refused the offer to serve if the amount of compensation was below what I deemed a minimum? I was not presented with that circumstance, but I do not think I would have.

Would this approach work for a full-time position? I see no reason why allowing the official church board to decide about matters of salary would differ for full-time versus part-time positions. If the parties involved are persons of integrity, then the decisions about compensation will be fair and equitable. After all, the persons on the board know what it costs to live in a certain area, and those costs vary depending on where the church is located. How can the associate know the amount of salary it will take to live in an area in which he or she has never lived? If the associate finds the salary too low for adequate support, the chosen standard of living may be too high and expectations may have to be adjusted.

Most salaries for associates are so low because the businessmen on the church board do not compare associate's salaries to those of industry. Matching salaries of paid staff with those outside the church with similar training and experience is normally not thought to be necessary. Churches look to other churches, but usually not to business or industry, for salary comparisons. In general, the salary for associates is lower and the time demands are higher when compared to business. Church-staff members are expected to sacrifice for the Lord's work.

Another reason for low salaries is that the church is expecting the paid staff to contribute "service-in-kind" to support the church. Anytime a businessman gives time or expertise to the church, it is a form of contribution to the church. This service-in-kind is thought by church board members to be necessary for everyone in the church, including the paid staff members. That is why most church staff members are busy many more hours per week than an hourly worker in business or industry. If the senior pastor is addicted to work, then the same is expected from the associates. Everyone is expected to do his or her part to support the church.

There are differing attitudes toward money that will, of course, affect the handling of salary and benefits. The first of these attitudes is that of the person who hoards money. They will save every bit possible, spending only what is necessary. This group would avoid most kinds of debt. Another kind of attitude toward money is that of the monk. They spend only what is necessary, but they do not hoard money. This person is called a monk because money is thought of as somehow tainted and worldly. Money is used, but not enjoyed. They will not enter into many debts either because monks should not have many worldly possessions. A third kind of attitude toward money is that of the spender who finds it difficult to save and often will be in debt. Money is freely distributed with little thought given to the future. Money is simply a means to an end and not carefully controlled.

These attitudes will certainly affect the associate's perspective on salary and benefits. The hoarder would very likely request a salary raise and put it in savings when it comes. The monk will probably not ask for a raise and if it does come, will feel it is not deserved. The spender will probably request more salary in order to pay the pesky bills that never seem to get paid off.

The issue of salary becomes more complex when those in charge of distributing the associate's salary (usually a committee) have different attitudes toward money among themselves. What if the associate is a spender and the committee members are all monks? If the associate is married and the two spouses have different attitudes toward money, it only exacerbates the problem of financial control. Monks find it easy to exhort spenders to form a budget and live by it. Hoarders will find it difficult to purchase even the necessities.

My wife and I have concluded that we are monks when it comes to money. So after thirty-five years of ministry, it does not matter much what the salary and benefits are for my ministry. Every new ministry I have gone to has paid a lower salary than the previous place of service. In good monklike fashion, we did not think this would lead to financial suicide, nor was it the height of stupidity. As Paul, I have learned "the secret of being content in any and every situation" (Phil. 4:12) and "godliness with contentment is great gain" (1 Tim. 6:6). Contentment for monks is not as difficult as it is for spenders or hoarders.

Conclusion

A few of the issues for an associate to consider in a relationship with the senior pastor of a church are assessing integrity, authority and power, communication patterns, and salary and benefits. The more that can be discovered about this crucial relationship before accepting the call, the better. Not all can be discovered before the call, but it is important to know what to look for, so that the associate is not surprised when it is found. The first-chair player has a very important role in the ministry of the associate, and the associate would be very wise to recognize that fact and learn to work with the senior pastor so they can develop into all that God wants them to be. Beautiful music comes no other way.

Discussion Questions

Use these questions privately or in a group, such as a church staff, to apply the points made in this chapter.

1. How would you assess the level of integrity in the lives of members of your church staff, including yourself? Are you pleased with what you found?

2. How could you discuss the issue of integrity with members of your church staff without judging or condemning anyone?

3. Do you practice a level of communication in your church staff that could be characterized as deep, personal, and meaningful? If not, what can be done to change communication patterns?

4. What events or situations illustrate for you the source of power and authority in your church staff? Is your perception matched by others on the staff?

5. How are salary and benefits of the pastoral staff determined? Is this process open to members of the staff? Should the process be open in your situation?

6. Do you see yourself primarily as a hoarder, monk, or spender when you evaluate your attitude toward money? How does your attitude affect your level of contentment with your salary?

7. Do you agree that the relationship between the associate and the senior pastor is the most important human relationship in regard to the effectiveness (success and longevity) of the associate? Why or why not?

CHAPTER SEVEN

How Should I Play with the Other Players?
(Other Pastoral Staff)

In any orchestra, the other players are very important to the type of sound that is produced. If the ensemble is a trumpet trio, it is a very different sound than if the ensemble is a string quartet. In a small orchestra, it is crucial to have a well-selected group of instruments in order to have a nicely balanced and well-rounded sound. The smaller the ensemble, the more important each of the other players is. Three violins might be fine for some occasions, but they cannot play the parts assigned to other instruments. Some musicians might be given a solo part for a time and then play backup at other times. How shall an associate cooperate with the other players on the church staff so beautiful music can be heard?

Common Ground

It is important to remember that pastoral staff members usually have more in common with others in the associate role than with the senior pastor. If the church staff is large and has more than one associate, staff members will share many of the same problems and joys. They can rejoice and commiserate together, which can provide them with a common ground for fellowship. Times of fellowship, however, should not degrade into pity parties or opportunities to tear down the senior pastor or other members of the staff. Fellowship with other staff members can provide enough of a similar experience to give them all common ground. After all, the best communication is between those who share something in common.

If there are no other associates on the church staff, associates in other churches or parachurch organizations can provide that kind of camaraderie. It is especially important that meetings for fellowship with those outside the church not become centered on gossip, but the common experiences of associates can provide a kind of support that is important. It is vital to understand what is really going on among the church staff members with regard to hierarchy and competition.

Hierarchy

The ideal is that all pastoral staff are equal—before the Lord, before the senior pastor, and before the church. The reality is that on most, if not all, pastoral staffs, a political subculture with a hierarchy exists. Every group of people will exhibit a kind of relationship with each other that can be called political. There is a ranking of members or a pecking order that becomes recognized, especially by those in the group. This hierarchy may be based on age or ministry experience, with the older associate having senior-associate status. The hierarchy may be based on length of service at a particular church— long-time associates may have out lasted the senior pastors and other associate staff members. The hierarchy may be based on one's ministry function or perception of authority in that function. The hierarchy might also be based on the perception of favoritism from those in authority.

For example, the staff member in charge of the music-worship program may have served the church for more years than the youth pastor has lived. It makes sense that the worship leader exhibit and expect more respect than the newcomer youth pastor. Or the long-time staff member might perceive that his or her authority and/or respect is being undercut. For example, the music-worship pastor may have had his program budget cut, while the youth pastor's budget was increased. The youth associate may be allowed to preach more frequently than the Christian education minister. The evangelism pastor may help lead the adult worship services more than has the children's associate. The visitation associate may be a very close friend of the senior pastor and the other associates feel left out. All of these, and many other possibilities, can become the basis for hurt feelings, friction, and conflict on the pastoral staff. Do staff members compete with each other?

Competition

One of the characteristics of American society is its penchant for competition. The church staff can be viewed as just another venue for rivalry. Rivalry and competition have permeated most of what Americans do on a day-to-day basis. From the time that we are little children we are taught that the important people in our society are those who are the winners. Losing should be avoided at all costs. Games become the motif for survival in our materialistic world. School becomes a place to compete with our classmates, and winning and losing is dependent on grade-point average and class rank. Athletics plays a huge role in our culture because winners and losers in sports are easily determined. The winners are given what our culture values—bragging rights and huge sums of money. In the workplace, coworkers become rivals for that advancement or promotion. Competition is very big in American life.

Is the motif of competition operational on the church staff? It is hard to live in a competitive culture for so many years and then simply put rivalry aside. The motif of cooperation that the musical ensemble suggests is much more in line with the biblical concept of the body of Christ. Does that mean that there are no games played on the church staff, games that would be expected if competition was the motif? One game in particular is called one-upmanship. This is when each staff member tries to outdo the others on the staff. Plans for activities can escalate until a specific church program becomes dominant. While this game should find no place in the pastoral ensemble, it may in reality be the standard procedure for church-staff relationships.

The cooperation motif of the ensemble recognizes that if one staff member does well, all should rejoice. If one is not doing well (however that is defined), the others on the church staff should rally around to help and encourage. The dog-eat-dog attitude of the world should not exist on a church staff. If a staff member goes out on a limb with a new program or idea, do the other staff members support, try to outdo, or worse, undercut the associate by criticizing the idea? The hierarchy of the staff will certainly affect the nature of competition on that church staff. There are other factors to be considered also. Let me illustrate some other factors by using two different case studies.

Case Study One

In one church where I served as the minister of Christian education and youth, a part-time music director led a youth choir. The choir was very well received by the congregation and plans were made to take the youth choir on a short tour to perform at churches in the surrounding area. The choir needed special outfits and the whole operational expense for the mini tour was outside the annual budget. I, as the full-time minister of Christian education and youth, was invited to go along on the tour to serve as a chaperone but had little part in the leadership of the choir. After all, that was the domain of the youth-choir director.

The youth choir grew in popularity and developed a life of its own apart from the youth program. The choir had Bible studies, worship and special prayer times, outreach activities, and many elements that the regular youth program had. As the program became more structured in the youth choir, there were inevitable conflicts between the youth-choir activities and the regular youth activities. The youth-choir rehearsal conflicted with the youth Bible study and most all of the youth opted for the more exciting youth choir. As the Christian education and youth minister, I was criticized because the youth program entailed little more than the youth choir. The implication was that there was little need for a full-time minister of Christian education and youth. Didn't the youth choir fulfill the purpose of the youth program?

This situation created a real difficulty in the working relationship between me and the youth-choir leader. I felt that the problem was an out-of-balance youth program. How could the youth choir become the whole youth program? Who was in charge of the overall youth program, and what role should the youth choir and its director play in the youth ministry? I felt that I was on the outside looking in on the youth program. The youth, their parents, the deacons, and other church leaders seemed to be of the opinion that the choir was the center of ministry for the youth and was the primary activity through which the youth ministered. Whenever the youth choir needed money for some project, it became available from the board of trustees of the church. When the youth minister needed money for a youth-ministry project, money was not available. These conflicts only exacerbated the conflict between me and my fellow staff member. How could such a conflict be resolved?

Conflict Resolution: The Need

After praying about a situation it should become obvious that, before any progress can be made, the need for resolution of the conflict must be present. The example mentioned above did not allow an overall youth ministry that was well balanced and that met the needs of all the youth. For example, should every young person be in the youth choir? How could a well-balanced youth program meet the needs of all youth, while allowing the youth-choir program to be developed? Was the perception that the youth choir dominated the youth program an accurate assessment? Was the conflict centered on the program for youth or was it actually a matter of leader pride? Had I been one-upped? As the person officially in charge of the youth program, I felt a great need for resolution of this problem and took it before the Lord in prayer.[1]

An initial step in resolving a conflict is to identify the issue or issues. One leader may not know how the other is feeling and may not be aware of a problem at all, especially if things are going smoothly for him or her. Identifying the issue or issues should not be done in an accusatory fashion. The leaders should not blame each other for the perceived problem. Rather, the approach should prayerfully focus on the resultant feelings about the situation, specifically the feelings of oneself. If I had started out by criticizing the youth-choir director for doing something wrong, his first reaction would have been to defend himself. He would say he was just doing his job to the best of his ability. He could easily say the problem was mine, not his. Once the cycle of accusation and defense begins, an argument ensues that usually has no resolution. Combatants will normally agree to disagree with each other. It is more helpful in resolving the conflict to appeal to the other person's compassion and mercy. When one tells of his frustration and hurt, the other usually responds by showing concern. If the need for resolution cannot be established, any subsequent steps are worthless. Do not proceed until it is agreed that there is a problem, but do not assess blame. Now the discussion is ready to move on to the next step.

Conflict Resolution: Willingness

The second step is to establish a commitment to resolve the conflict. The discussion must move from, "Yes, we have a problem" to "I am willing to work on the solution to this problem." It is necessary for both parties in the conflict to express a willingness to resolve the conflict, or to own the problem. In my case, an appeal to the best interests of those who are served (the youth themselves) or to the program as a whole (the total youth program) would help to create that commitment to fix the problem. It may help if an appeal to friendship or fellowship between the primary combatants in the conflict is felt and responded to by the other party. As long as there is unwillingness to do anything about the conflict, there is no need created to resolve it. Sometimes a crisis precipitates the needed willingness to resolve the conflict. If everything is going smoothly, why try to fix what is not broken?

Conflict Resolution: Options

The next step to resolve conflict is to review the options available. If there is a desire to find a workable resolution to the conflict, finding options makes sense. Bringing others into the situation at this point may be helpful. Having many minds working on the problem helps to create more possibilities. With more minds working on the possibilities, more creative thinking can take place; more ways can be discovered to resolve the problem. Many ideas can be generated, and if they are not immediately evaluated for their usefulness, they can serve as springboards to other ideas that might have more benefit. Nothing should be held back at this stage in the process. The purpose of this step is to provide as many options as possible, not to evaluate how helpful any of them might be.

The next step is to review the list of options and group them into categories. Some ideas might be similar and could be combined, and other ideas may seem to be more separate or individual. Some may be unworkable and need to be temporarily set aside. This is where the ideas are evaluated. Ownership of the ideas must be relinquished, because if an idea is rejected, it does not mean the person who suggested it is rejected. Having more people working on the evaluation of the ideas is helpful when the process moves to the next step—to implement the idea or ideas selected.

Conflict Resolution: Implications

After the main categories have been established, the next step is to think through how each of the main categories of ideas could be carried out in reality. What would be the implications of each if they were activated in this situation? In my case, for example, if one of the groups of ideas centered around sharing the leadership of the choir with the minister of Christian education and youth, how might that be accomplished? One of the ideas might have been that the youth minister lead the Bible study or devotions for the youth choir. This idea could have been grouped with sharing leadership of the choir with the youth minister. It is here that the ideas are evaluated for practicality and feasibility. Another idea grouped with sharing leadership might be that the youth minister assist as sound technician or transportation coordinator. As the various groups of ideas are discussed, it will become clearer what will be easy to implement and what will be more difficult. It will become clear what needs to change in the situation in order for any of the ideas to be accomplished.

Conflict Resolution: Implementation

The next step is to select one of the ideas or a group of ideas. There may be many ideas that might work and that might be useable to resolve the perceived conflict. The idea that is selected may be the one that all parties of the resolution team can agree with, rather than any idea that was the brainchild of any specific person. The good of the whole situation must be more important than any personal agenda brought into the resolution process. Putting the idea into the form of a goal helps carry out the next step in the resolution of conflict. After an idea is selected, action steps for implementation can be designed.

Action steps should be stated in concrete terms and with a schedule for implementation. It does little good to agree to do something about the conflict and then have no plan to accomplish it. Action steps are simply sequential procedures that fulfill the agreed upon goal. Action steps should be assigned to a person to carry out by a certain date. Here again, it is good to have more people involved to help carry out the action steps.

Conflict Resolution: Evaluation

The last stage in this process is to evaluate progress after a period of time. Perhaps one of the action steps could be to meet again in six months to evaluate how well the other action steps were implemented. The process may need some fine-tuning, or there may be new conflicts that need resolution by then. A process for the conflict resolution has been established, and hopefully the next conflict will be resolved smoothly and equitably.

Conflict Resolution: Application

I wish I could report that the situation described above with the youth-choir director was resolved according to the steps I have outlined. There were attempts at building a relationship through family get-togethers, but there was no actual confrontation of the issues I was feeling. I guess I hoped the whole thing would resolve itself. It, of course, did not resolve by itself, and I continued to feel frustrated by what I perceived as the overly dominant role of the youth choir in the total youth program. I did volunteer to assist with the youth choir, but the activities I contributed to the youth choir did not change the overall place of the youth choir as the most popular and dominant feature in the youth program. I did learn lessons about myself and about the importance of conflict resolution on the church staff.

Case Study Two

In another church where I worked with another associate pastoral staff member, we did experience a smooth-working relationship. I was the minister of education and he was the full-time youth pastor. This youth pastor had followed a very popular predecessor who had served at the church for several years. After a period of weeks, it became apparent that attendance at the Wednesday night program, developed by the previous youth director, was declining. I felt the need to do something about it. The situation could have been assessed to be the fault of the new youth pastor. Unfavorable comparisons to the previous youth director could have been made, and the new youth pastor could have been hurt or felt unfairly treated. It was possible that we could have forced him to resign or that he would have concluded that he needed to resign. The cycle of accusation and defense would have resolved nothing. What did happen was the result of following the steps I described above. We prayed together about the Wednesday youth program and agreed that there was a problem, and we expressed a willingness to work out a solution. Several college- and career-aged people were included in the discussions. Options were generated and a new plan for Wednesday night was designed and implemented. Action steps were created and persons were assigned responsibilities to carry them out. We set a schedule for the new program and followed the schedule. The result was that the new Wednesday night program created more excitement than the old program, and attendance shot up higher than it had ever been.

Conflict: Avoid or Attack?

It may be important to discuss the factors involved in the decision of whether to avoid or attack the conflict. Why did I not deal with the conflict I felt with the youth choir director? Why did I take the initiative with the youth pastor in the second situation? There may be many reasons for a member on a pastoral staff to decide to proceed with or to avoid a confrontation with another staff member, but I hesitate to speculate. Let me say why I think I did not confront the director of the youth choir and why I did the youth pastor. Perhaps you can relate to some of these reasons.

One reason I avoided confrontation was because I thought if I did tell the youth-choir director how I felt, he would be unsympathetic. I assumed he was in a higher position of authority (if not power) with the church and with the members of the youth group. He had been at the church longer than I, he was well liked, and his program was going very well. I assumed that he had little need to resolve the conflict that I perceived existed.

The confrontation with the youth pastor was based on a common perception of need. We both recognized attendance was dropping and that the new youth pastor did not possess the personality or the skills of the previous youth pastor. There was no blame assigned; there was a rather objective discussion of the facts. Since I had been in my position longer than the new youth pastor, I may have operated from a stronger base of authority and power. It was to the advantage of both of us to agree that something needed to be done.

Another reason I avoided confrontation with the youth-choir director was because I felt insecure. We had just moved to this church from thousands of miles away, and we had not established deep friendships or alliances yet. The senior pastor had just resigned, and I was expected to carry on his duties as well as my own. I was feeling pressure from the board and other church leaders to turn around the plummeting attendance at the worship services and the declining offerings. I was not feeling particularly confident or assured. My personal insecurity was at an all-time high. Confronting the youth-choir director did not seem wise when I was feeling ineffective in most every other area of my ministry.

I did not feel insecure with the youth pastor. In this situation, I was higher on the staff hierarchy because I had been on the staff longer and had many more years experience than he. I also had a better personal relationship with the youth pastor through day-to-day contact. We met every day to share our lives, pray together, and to discuss and plan upcoming events that related to the youth. Perhaps I had learned from my previous experience about the importance of dealing with issues quickly as well as the absurdity of delay and/or avoidance.

Another reason I avoided a confrontation with the youth-choir director was that I feared the outcome. Once the conflict was out in the open, I thought the youth and perhaps the whole church would take sides. The divisiveness that might result would be primarily my fault since I raised the issue, and I did not want responsibility for dividing any element of the church. There were other issues in the church as a whole that caused me to wonder if the conflict with the youth-choir director was worth the effort. There were enough reasons for division in our church without me tossing another one on the pile. The future looked grim enough without providing another reason for another section of the church to break away. If battle lines were drawn, I assumed I would be on the losing side. I assumed the worst about any possible outcome of confronting the youth-choir director.

The outcome of the confrontation with the youth pastor was unknown at the beginning, but there was a confidence that somehow we could work it out. I felt that our personal relationship was strong enough (even though it was young) to weather the storm of confrontation. Whatever the outcome, the assurance existed in both of us that it had to be better than the alternative—a continued decline in attendance in the Wednesday night program.

One obvious difference between the two situations was that I had little contact with the youth-choir director and daily personal contact with the youth pastor. The personal relationship was much stronger with the youth pastor because of the increased time we spent together.

Whether you can relate to any of these reasons or not, associates often find excuses for inaction when it comes to resolving a conflict with another associate. I realize that I tend to excessively analyze situations, so it is easy for me to think of possible negative outcomes for conflict situations. Did any of those negative outcomes actually happen? I did stay in the church with the youth-choir director for two and one-half years and the conflict was not resolved. Other and much larger conflicts arose in the church that drew my attention away from the youth choir. There were church divisions, but it was not over the youth choir. Would things have turned out differently if I had confronted the youth-choir director? That is hard to say, but I know I would have achieved a much better working relationship with him had I followed the steps outlined above.

As a result of dealing with the youth pastor and the Wednesday night program, we developed a stronger personal relationship than before and experienced about four years of exciting ministry together. It was definitely worth it to deal with the issue early on in our relationship.

Conclusion

One of the hallmarks of longevity on the part of associate staff members is the ability to resolve conflicts. The other members of the pastoral staff have an important role to play in the ministry of the associate. Getting along with others cannot be limited to the senior pastor or the official church board. Associates cannot afford to exist in a lone-ranger mode. The associate must be ready and willing to work out the bumps in the relationship with other staff members. *When* conflicts arise (not *if* they arise), avoidance will do nothing to help the situation. In fact, things will only get worse. Some people even experience physical symptoms because of conflict. Working out the problems must be the *modus operandi* of the associate. It is the only way for beautiful music to emanate from the church staff.

Discussion Questions

Use these questions privately or in a group, such as a church staff, to apply the points made in this chapter.

1. Can you give examples of any common ground you may share with other members of your pastoral staff? You may use church staff members from other churches or parachurch organizations if necessary.

2. In what way does the political hierarchy function in your church staff? Is anyone thought of as possessing more authority than the others? If so, why?

3. Is competition the general motif of your church staff? What are the indicators that it is, or the definite reasons that lead you to think it is not?

4. Are any competitive games being played by members of your church staff? Any one-upmanship happening?

5. If you are experiencing a conflict with another staff member right now, is there recognition of the conflict by both persons? If not, what needs to be done to bring it out in the open?

6. Is there a willingness to come to some kind of resolution of the conflict, or have you been stranded by the other party to the conflict? (It's not my problem.)

7. What do you think about the approach to resolving the conflict with a particular person that involves others in the process? Would that benefit or hinder the resolution of the conflict?

8. Can you disconnect yourself from the solution to the conflict that you think is best, or are you wedded to it? Would you be offended if your idea was tossed out and someone else's idea used?

9. Are you willing to do what is necessary to resolve the conflict with another staff member? How do you know that you are? How do you know that you are not willing, and what will it take to help you become willing?

10. What are some reasons of your own that have caused you to avoid confrontation, to avoid attempting to resolve personal conflicts?

11. Besides the steps in this chapter, what else would you suggest for resolving conflicts with your colleagues on the pastoral staff?

CHAPTER EIGHT

How Should I Play with Those Not Paid?
(General Church Members)

Members of a professional orchestra normally are given a stipend for their services. The pay might be based on individual performances or on a single season or a contract of several years. Being paid to perform is usually what distinguishes the professional from the amateur. Bringing a performer into the orchestra who is nonpaid would be highly unusual. Prodigies would receive some payment for their services and well-known artists could command large sums for their performances.

Associate staff members who play their instruments within the context of a local church are similar to those who play in an orchestra. The difference is that the church uses mostly unpaid staff. The relationship of the paid staff with the unpaid staff is the focus of this chapter.

It may be helpful to clarify who exactly is the church staff. If the associate thinks he or she alone is the church staff, and the general church membership is the primary audience for the performance of the associate's ministry, he or she is mistaken. Scripture tells us that every member of the church is a worker and therefore a part of the church staff (Rom. 12:4–5 and 1 Cor. 12:14). Every believer is given spiritual gifts (Rom. 12:6–8 and 1 Cor. 12:7) for the common good. Is this work just for a few?

The work of ministry is done by each of the members. Ephesians 4:11–13 is clear that people with certain gifts are to equip the rest so they might do the work of service. Everyone who is a believer is a worker and should be considered a part of the church staff. Some of the church staff are paid, most are not paid for their services. Every member has a gift package that is to be utilized in service to God. Ideally, no one need volunteer for service because everyone should, by virtue of his or her relationship to Christ, already be an integral part of the orchestra called the church staff. Therefore, I am going to refer to church workers as unpaid staff and vocational ministers as paid staff. How should the paid staff and the unpaid staff think about each other?

Some instruments in a volunteer orchestra may have to be augmented, thus specially enlisted and paid so the sound may be fuller and more complete. The unpaid players are still expected to play their best, but a paid associate staff member may have a unique contribution to make to the local ministry orchestra. There may be members of the church who have spiritual gifts that have been expressed in a unique way through volunteer service. These laypeople may have been invited to join the paid church staff in order to free them from other responsibilities and allow them to focus on the ministry. An associate from the outside with skills not evident in the local church ministry may be asked to join with the other members of the orchestra. How does paying someone to do ministry affect the members of the church staff orchestra who are not paid?

Reaction of Unpaid Staff

It is possible that the unpaid staff member might react with great enthusiasm to the news that a paid associate is coming to the church. The unpaid staff might feel that the church should have the benefit of a specialist for a particular ministry. The unpaid may have been lobbying for the paid staff member for some time, so the addition will be welcome indeed. The unpaid may be looking forward to having a colleague with whom they can fellowship in and through the specific ministry they both serve. All reactions, however, might not be positive.

One of the reactions might be resentment toward the paid associate from the unpaid. After all, wasn't the unpaid serving in this ministry first? Did the leadership of the church find the service of the unpaid lacking in some way? Why was a replacement brought in to do the job the unpaid staff had been doing all along? In addition to feeling replaced, the unpaid may resent that he or she is now expected to support the paid staff member in the ministry area. The unpaid might feel indignation toward the paid staff—if the unpaid staff was not good enough, then why support the person who was brought into this ministry to do the work that the unpaid had been doing? Why does the new paid staff person receive so much attention when the unpaid has been serving faithfully without fanfare for so many years?

Another negative reaction of the unpaid to the paid might be withdrawal from ministry. The unpaid may have been smelling the fumes of burnout for some time and thus take the opportunity of the coming of a paid associate to quit. The unpaid may reason, If the paid staff member is uniquely suited to do this ministry, then why not drop out of service and allow the more skilled paid associate to do it? Withdrawal may not occur immediately upon the associate's arrival, but when it does occur, burnout or inadequacy may be the reasons given. Inadequacy on the part of the unpaid may not be true at all, but unfortunately, the unpaid staff may now feel it. How can the paid associate help to resolve these feelings and help retain current staff and even recruit more unpaid staff to meaningful ministry?

Role of the Unpaid

The role of the unpaid seems to be widely misunderstood in the church. Ephesians 4:11–13 is rather clear about who is to do the work of the ministry. It says that the saints are to do it, and the gifted people, such as pastors and teachers, are to equip them for the work of service. Why have the roles of the ministers and equippers seemingly been reversed? Why have the paid associates been expected to do the work of the ministry and the saints (general church members) been given a backseat kind of equipping task such as providing the support funds for ministry? Why have general church members been restricted from full participation in the church staff orchestra, even from playing an occasional solo?

I do not know of one Christian church, evangelical or mainline, that disagrees with the thought of Ephesians 4:11–13. That is, none would say that lay involvement is not a good thing. Senior pastors are for it, church boards are for it, associates are for it, and most, if not all, church members are for church-member involvement. In spite of all this outward support for full involvement of the laity, there are few churches who really practice it. I do not know of many churches where unpaid staff involvement is 100 percent of the congregation. There are few churches in which every believer has a meaningful ministry that matches his or her spiritual gifts, interests, and skills. There are, however, many churches that have large ministries that are built on many paid staff associates. Even in churches with large numbers of unpaid staff workers, the percentage of involvement is well below fifty percent of the whole congregation. Observations like this would lead one to ask why the number of unpaid staff in the ministry of the local church is not higher. Why is there not full employment?

Organization and Organism

If the local church is compared to secular business, a group of local believers might be considered an organization, similar to other not-for-profit organizations. The description of the church found in the Bible, however, is less like an organization and more like an organism. The church of the Bible, and especially of the New Testament, is less like a corporation and more like a family and like a human body. The church as an organization would have a hierarchy of leaders that plans what and how something should be done. These plans can be new ministry ideas, programs, or emphases designed to meet the needs of the local church. The organizational leaders set the budget and recruit leaders to carry out the plan.

The church as an organism has no hierarchy except the head, which Paul tells us is Christ (Eph. 2:20–22). In an organism, every part of the body takes direction from the head, and while each part has various functions all are equal. When each part of the organism does what it is intended and gifted to do, the various plans for ministry grow. Every part of the organism is important and none more important than the other (1 Cor. 12:20–26). How does this affect the paid-unpaid issue?

Those churches that operate more like an organization will tend to hire specially skilled associate staff from outside the local church. The leaders of this type of nonprofit corporation will determine the responsibilities of the new staff member and make a list of qualifications for this ministry. Unpaid staff from within the local church may be used at first, but after the program grows and becomes more complex, it will often be determined that a more professional leader is needed. That person may be recruited from within the church, but usually someone is sought who has more experience with larger ministries, and those persons are usually from the outside.

Those churches that operate more like an organism will tend to prefer unpaid staff. When paid staff becomes necessary, the organism church will prefer those who have developed from within their fellowship. The unpaid staff will tend to be the norm in the organism church because there will likely be few paid staff, such as the pastor. If everyone is expected to serve, the thought of hiring someone from the outside is seldom considered seriously. Organism churches tend to be smaller, but the percentage of active unpaid staff involvement is much higher than the organization church. From the standpoint of lay involvement, the organism church seems to have the edge. Why aren't all churches more organism than organization? If only it were that easy.

Churches may begin life functioning in organism-like fashion, but after a while, they become increasingly organized. In fact, the older, and usually the larger, the church becomes the more organized it has to be. The church of fifty or fewer that operated in the beginning as an organism can no longer do that when it is five hundred or more in size. Organizational structure is required to insure that all of the programs and activities in the church run smoothly. Functioning as an organism, however, may still be valued in the larger church and this is manifested when new ministries develop in organism fashion. A subgroup of the larger church, such as the youth ministry, might develop an organismic ministry within the organization. Generally speaking, however, functioning as an organization becomes the way in which the larger church has to operate due to its size.

The church that is older but smaller than it used to be will find particular struggles with its organization. The larger organizational structure is not needed by the now smaller church, but it will be very difficult to reshape to the needs of the now-smaller church. Tradition will make the termination of certain, ineffective programs very difficult. Moving to a more organism-oriented church will be difficult, too, because of the many years of doing business in a certain way. The formerly large church organization that is now smaller, faces some unique challenges in staffing their ministries.

It should be said that no church is totally organization or totally organism; there are elements of both in most churches. It is probably easier to think of organization and organism as a continuum rather than an either-or choice. The enlistment and recruitment of nonpaid staff will be approached differently, depending on whether organism or organization is dominant. My warning is, be careful before you decide which your church is.

Case Study

I was asked to consider working part-time as an associate pastor of Christian education in a local church that was about eleven years old. I agreed to lead an hour seminar for four consecutive weeks on planning what a Christian education (CE) ministry in that specific church would look like. While I did this, the church could get a look at me and I could evaluate them. Everyone in the church was invited. During the first three weeks the meetings were well-attended and excitement was high. I did not see evidence of heavy emphasis on organization in the CE program or the church as a whole. I concluded that the church leaned toward functioning as an organism. I was excited about the potential of leading a team of committed and enthusiastic people who would be a vital part of the planning and implementation process of the CE ministry. The fourth and last session of the seminar was Mother's Day and attendance dropped to one-third of the previous three weeks. It so happened that I planned to ask for a commitment that final day to carry out the CE goals we had agreed on the previous three weeks. The result was that sign-ups for commitment to serve were much lower in number than I had expected. In fact, sign-ups were lower than we needed to carry out the plans that had been made together. Now what should I do?

In spite of the low number of sign-ups, my wife and I agreed to take the part-time CE position in the church. My thoughts were: (1) that I had interpreted the drop in attendance the last week as the fault of the holiday, (2) that the excitement I saw in the previous three weeks would be the norm, and (3) that the church was more organism-like than organization-like, even though it numbered about four hundred in attendance at the time. As time passed, I realized the error of my thinking.

It was true that the church did have some elements of organism and was less organized compared to churches of a similar size. I also became aware that what had worked well when the church was smaller would not work any longer. The function of organism, such as everyone's having a part in the decision-making process, was no longer possible. When I organized my work in CE and carried it out, I noticed the comments made about it. Things were said to me such as, "We are finally getting organized around here," as if that were a good thing. I realized that some (if not many) wanted more organization and structure in the church rather than less and that my perception of the church's tending toward organism was much less than I had thought. As time went on, I concluded that the church was depending more and more on the paid staff (my wife and I) to do the CE ministry.

Motivation

When it comes to involvement of unpaid staff in the ministry of the local church, the issue of motivation must be addressed. It is no surprise that the level of motivation for lay service in our churches varies widely. Some workers, albeit the minority, seem to be indefatigable and seem to thrive on ministry. These workhorses are super involved and can be depended on to always be there. Then there are some who have no time at all for ministry service in the local church and are therefore totally uninvolved. They receive ministry from the church, but do not give it to anyone else. These depend on the paid staff for the work of ministry to be done. The majority of the church body is somewhere in the middle, but probably leans toward the uninvolved side. What causes some unpaid staff to serve as if their life and perhaps salvation depend on it? What motivates unpaid staff to serve the Lord at all in the local church?

The culture of the 1990s has certainly affected the church when it comes to service. The quantity of volunteerism to all kinds of unpaid community service in America seems to be high. In 1995, ninety-three million adult Americans volunteered, performing an estimated 20.3 billion hours of service—an average of 4.2 hours per week per person. More people volunteer for religious organizations than for any other type of organization. Half of those questioned said they volunteered because they gain a sense of satisfaction by volunteering.[1] It seems that the motivation for volunteer service has shifted somewhat. In the past, people might have based their service to the community on altruistic notions of giving back. A church worker could have based her service on her love for the Lord Jesus Christ, the perceived good of the church, or, perhaps, duty. Some may serve for these or other noble reasons, but many today serve because of what they will receive from it. The me generation asks, What's in it for me? If, for instance, a man agrees to serve in an unpaid position, whether with the Red Cross or the local church, his motivation will likely be based partially or mostly on a reason related to personal gain. Serving as a volunteer might look good on a résumé. How can a person work for the glory of God and be doing it for personal reasons?

It does little good to decry the state of our culture and its effect on unpaid church staff. Telling people they are selfish and that their service should be based on higher and nobler reasons will not help to create more workers. Pointing out selfishness to uninvolved workers usually creates guilt and guilt is a terrible basis for service. Guilt-ridden workers usually do not last long in ministry if they start at all. It is better to recognize the situation we are in and work with it. If people need to feel that their service has a personal return attached to it, why not emphasize the personal rewards that are ours when we serve the living God? Does not Scripture describe rewards that the believer will receive for effective service for Christ?

Rewards

Future rewards are described in Scripture such as Christ's words, "Well done, good and faithful servant" (Matt. 25:21), and the book of Hebrews tells of our entering into a future, eternal rest (4:1). Paul instructs us to serve as if we were building with gold, silver, and precious stones rather than with wood, hay, or stubble (1 Cor. 3:12–15). Paul says that if we do, we will receive a reward. There is the so-called bema seat judgment mentioned in 2 Corinthians 5:10 where believers will be recompensed for what they have done. Can there be any greater reward than hearing, "Well done, good and faithful servant"?

These rewards are future and some will still ask if there is any scriptural description of a present reward for serving Jesus. A delayed reward relegated to heaven is fine, but what about the here and now? Is there anything that can be received now as a direct result of serving Christ rather than waiting for our heavenly reward? We may even forget about any future reward because of its distance from us. Modern unpaid staff workers need to know if there is a present reward for serving Christ.

The old song says, "There is joy in serving Jesus," but many have either lost the joy, or they never had it in the first place. Are the rather ephemeral qualities such as joy, peace, love, and so forth the only present rewards the believer receives from Christian service? I believe that these inner and nontangible qualities are the very rewards God offers and, more importantly, the very rewards each believer needs. Let me explain by means of examining a theory of why we act the way we do.

Influencing Service

A brief definition of the theory of behaviorism goes as follows. Our behavior is basically a reaction to a stimulus in our environment.[2] When the stimulus and reaction are useful to the organism, the behavior is repeated. When the organism finds the process useless or distasteful, the behavior is avoided. The behavior that is followed by satisfaction will more likely recur; that which is accompanied by discomfort will be less likely to occur.[3] Behavioral psychologists divide all behavior in two broad classes: respondent and operant. Respondent behavior is primarily controlled by events that precede it, while operant behavior is primarily controlled by events that follow it.[4] Respondent behavior is passive: the environment acts on the organism to produce a response. In operant behavior, however, the organism acts on the environment to produce a change, and this change is followed by a reinforcing stimulus.[5] How is a Christian worker's serving behavior affected by reinforcement?

The behavioristic theory says behavior will be strengthened by two procedures: positive and negative reinforcement. When an operant (behavior) is followed by the presentation of a stimulus, and an increase in the frequency of the operant (behavior) is observed, the process is called positive reinforcement. When an operant (behavior) is followed by the removal of a stimulus, and an increase in the frequency of the response is observed, the process is called negative reinforcement.

Weakening the operant (behavior) may also be accomplished in two ways. If a response decreases in frequency when it is followed by a particular stimulus, the process is called punishment. A second procedure for weakening responses involves removing a stimulus following the response; the most common term for this process is called response

111

cost. Both punishment and response cost result in a decrease in the frequency of a performance.[6]

Understanding this bit of behavioral theory could make a difference in understanding how the motivation of workers functions. Associate staff members who are paid are continually attempting to enlist workers. Knowing what motivates people to serve in the local church could be a big step in increasing lay involvement. If attempts are made to influence the serving behavior of others, it is only wise to understand what causes others to react in positive ways and attempt to work with it.

For example, positive reinforcement (praise) of a worker or his or her ministry is far more effective in influencing the person to keep serving in that ministry than no reinforcement or negative reinforcement. The praise should not become excessive or be insincere, but recognizing what others are doing and thanking them for it will have a positive affect on the workers. A word spoken or a note of appreciation sent can be very helpful. Public recognition should be given more than just at an annual thank-you banquet at the end of the year. Individuals or departments might be regularly highlighted before the whole church. Of the four types of influence we can have on others, positive reinforcement is by far the most effective. Regular meetings with the staff should be positive and should focus on what is being accomplished for good.

The source of a Christian's joy is not obtained from other human beings, but it should be clear that anyone's Christian service is affected by how others react to what they do for Christ. For example, if I am praised for my work for Christ, I will feel affirmed and my spiritual gift will be confirmed. The body of Christ has recognized the service and offers a word of thanks, encouragement, or support for it. Positive and negative reinforcement supports my serving behavior and brings a fulfillment to my service. We all need this kind of joy as we are affirmed in our being used for the edification of the body of Christ. If we show appreciation for a person's service, that person will experience more joy and will want to stay.

Negative reinforcement can be used to encourage workers in the fulfillment of their ministry of service. If the paid staff member sees her ministry as being an equipper, then it is obvious that providing assistance for workers is part of her task. Removing barriers the workers may be experiencing becomes an encouragement. Supplying needed equipment or supplies inspires workers to continue. Getting curriculum materials to lay workers in plenty of time so they can prepare adequately is a help to the motivation of workers. Listening provides many opportunities for this kind of influence.

It does not seem appropriate for punishment to be considered as a way to influence Christian workers. One reason might be that punishment is the least effective way to influence long-term serving behavior. It would be wise, however, to evaluate whether there might be inadvertent things being done that result in unwanted results. Is there a reason for the rapid and continual turnover of staff in a particular department? There should be no intentional forms of punishment in the relationships between paid and unpaid staff, but there might be unintentional forms. Increasing the quality of ministry and the number of those serving is positive, but punishment reduces these results. Is there anything being done that lessens quality or reduces the staff size?

For example, praising one staff member and not another might be viewed as a form of punishment by the slighted. Punishment might include chastisement for the perceived failure of a worker, even if the comment is offered in jest. If there is criticism of the person's service, the worker can be devastated. The criticism may be intended to be constructive or helpful, but it may not be received that way. Workers can feel they are not good enough for the high demands of service in the church. The offhanded comment may confirm the suspicion that they were inadequate in some way.

It is probably that the unpaid staff frequently evaluates the response cost for their Christian service. As a process that reduces positive behavior, response cost is the removal of some positive factor the worker has been anticipating. For example, if the thank-you banquet is canceled with no explanation after being held every year for the last decade, the cancellation might reduce the good-serving behavior of some workers. They do not serve because of the banquet, but the removal of it may lead some to question the basis for their motivation. The absence of thanks from those served or from those supervising the ministry might lead to less-enthusiastic serving. Response cost, as in the removal of something expected, will cause some workers to not only feel discouraged but also to feel unworthy of any kind of recognition for their service. What about those who serve as critics of those serving?

Critics

Since so many in the church prefer to serve God in an advisory capacity, I have a theory about why criticism abounds in the church. If a person is spiritually gifted in a certain area, he or she may feel especially sensitive to the expression of particular spiritual gift(s). For example, if a man is spiritually gifted in administration but is not using that gift, the thing in the church that will frustrate him the most is the way the church is administered. I have noticed that those with a specific spiritual gift can ignore the way every other gift is expressed, except the one they possess. There is no spiritual gift of criticism, but since so many practice it, I have concluded that those who criticize see a particular weakness because of their particular strengths. So how shall the critic be handled?

The way that critics can be managed most effectively is to encourage them to get involved in the area they have criticized. Tell them they may be gifted in this area because they have a vision that enables them to see what could be done and what must be done to improve it. Criticism might be a veiled request on the critic's part to be asked to be involved in that particular ministry. A recent poll of American adults who volunteered revealed the biggest reason they did so was because they were asked.[7]

If the critic says no after you ask him or her to participate, then point out that he or she has no right to criticize the ones who are doing their best. Those serving should receive our thanks and appreciation, not our criticism. If people have the nerve to criticize those actually doing a particular ministry, then an associate should have enough nerve to challenge the critic to get involved in that ministry personally. Why shouldn't the gifted rather than just the willing be doing the ministry?

Spiritual Gifting

The most crucial theological issue related to unpaid service in the church is that of spiritual gifts. Many churches teach about spiritual gifts, such as which gifts there are, which ones they believe are operative today, and which are not. They even teach that every member of the body of Christ has received a spiritual gift. Some even lead their members to discover what spiritual gift or gifts each may have. Unfortunately, that is not enough.

The key to mobilizing the unpaid staff in the work of the ministry is the implementation of spiritual gifts. To help people identify their spiritual gift and then not allow an opportunity for them to use the gifts in the local church only creates more critics. Most church members know that they should employ their spiritual gifts for the edification of the body of Christ. Many also know what spiritual gift(s) they have, but most do not use them. Thus, this fabulous resource goes untapped; unpaid staff go without a place of service.

Churches need to teach about spiritual gifts and then develop a way to enlist every member in doing something for God's kingdom that employs his or her spiritual gift. One way might be through a seminar. In one church, I was asked to lead a group to be mobilized into Christian service. Each person was asked to complete a spiritual-gift inventory[8] before the Saturday morning we met. At the seminar, the various spiritual gifts were explained and discussed. I asked those present to divide into their primary spiritual-gift group, with teachers in one group, helpers in another, administrators in another, and so forth. When everyone was seated in the new arrangement, they looked at each other with new eyes. Some were in the group that everyone who was present agreed they should be in. Others were in groups that shocked some of those present. Some, for example, scored themselves highest as possessing the teaching gift, yet they were not teaching. We discussed the implications of this new experiment with seating arrangement and concluded that some needed to change their ministries. Others needed to drop the activities they were doing that were not an expression of their spiritual gift. Some needed to become involved in ministries that utilized their spiritual gift. It was an illuminating experience.

There is no better time to present the opportunity for service in the church than at the new-member or the introduction-to-the-church class. People in these classes will be more willing to serve than at any other time during their membership. At the new-member class a spiritual-gift inventory could become a required element. The information from the inventory could be used to enlist or place every new member into a ministry that fulfills his or her spiritual gift(s) and meets the needs of the local church. One of the most highly developed programs for enlisting workers I have seen is called the Network Serving Seminar (Equipping Those Who Are Seeking to Serve). This was originally produced by and for the Willow Creek Community Church in South Barrington, Illinois.[9] A separate organization called Network now exists that provides a similar program for lay involvement in local church ministry.[10] Whether this or any other type of program is used, some plan must be followed to intentionally and systematically enlist workers until every member is active in service for the Lord Jesus Christ.

Conclusion

The associate's role with the unpaid staff is to serve as equipper so that there might be an ever-growing ensemble of players to carry on the work of ministry. Would it not be wonderful if every believer was motivated and actively involved in some type of Christian service based on the worker's spiritual gift, interest, and talents? The sound of such an orchestra would certainly wake up the entire world.

Discussion Questions

Use these questions privately or in a group, such as a church staff, to apply the points made in this chapter.

1. How does the unpaid staff feel toward the paid staff in your church? Were any resentful about the arrival of the paid staff member?

2. Have any unpaid staff left since the paid staff has come? Do you think it likely any more will leave? What can be done about it?

3. Do the people in your church feel the primary role of the paid staff is to equip people of the church to do the work of ministry? How do you know? What makes you think they do not?

4. Count the total number of possible positions of service that could be available in your church. Include every kind of ministry you can think of, even those you do not have right now. Compare that number to the total number of adults currently attending your church.

5. What do you conclude from your research for question four? Is there a place for everyone to serve if they want to serve? Or do you have far more places of service than persons available to fill them?

6. What percentage of your church could be called active in the work of ministry?

7. Is your church more like an organism or like an organization? What evidence makes you answer as you did?

8. Are there ways your organizational church can operate as an organism, either as a whole or in any of its subgroups?

9. Do you recognize any characteristics of me-ism in your church? Do people in your church serve primarily because of what is in it for them?

10. How is the issue of rewards (future and current) for Christian service handled in your church?

11. Which type of influence do you primarily use with unpaid workers? Positive reinforcement (praise), negative reinforcement (making service easier), punishment (chastisement for failure), or response cost (absence of something expected)? Any need for change?

12. How do you respond to the theory that explains why people become critics in the church?

13. Do you lead all of your people to find a ministry based on their spiritual gift, their interests, and talents? If yes, how? If no, what can you do to begin?

CHAPTER NINE

Is the Conductor Sympathetic?
(Boards and Committees)

The conductor is the most visible person in the orchestra, standing in front of all the players. The conductor waves his arms and, with the baton, directs the instrumentalists to play together. The conductor sets the tempo and cues various groups of instruments when to play. Some conductors are flamboyant and others are very staid and formal. It is the conductor's entrance that is greeted by applause and it is the conductor who takes the bows when the performance is over. The conductor usually rehearses the players before the performance, so each player knows how this conductor will direct the specific pieces of music. The conductor often explains the music to the audience.

The official board could be thought of as the conductor of the pastoral ensemble. Some may assert that it is the Lord who is the conductor of the church staff and it is he who should be followed, not the official board. While this is true in an abstract sense, it is the official board who ostensibly acts on the Lord's behalf with the church staff. It is the official board that does the screening and the interviewing of the associate staff. Depending on the polity of the church, it is the official board that either recommends to the church to call or extends the call themselves on behalf of the church. It is the board that sets the general responsibilities for each staff member. The official board might be called elders, overseers, deacons, or some other name, but it is this group that is responsible for the general oversight of the ministry of the staff. It is the board that often interprets the actions of the staff to the church. The associate must know how to relate to the members of the board. In other words, what is the level of sympathy or support the official board has toward the paid staff?

Relationship Types

There are various types of relationships an associate can have with the official board of the church. The first type of relationship is that

118

of a servant. The servant relationship seems to be quite logical because the board was directly involved, at least initially, in the call or hiring of the associate. It was the board that negotiated the ministry description for the associate. This is also normally the group that will hold the associate accountable for fulfilling the ministry description. It is, therefore, only fitting that some associates seek to serve the board according to the understanding that has been mutually agreed to. This type of relationship has definite biblical support.

A second kind of relationship is that of a leader. The associate assumes the position of leader of the board. An associate will not likely assume leadership of the official board, however, unless he is a general associate and there is no senior pastor on staff at the time. The usual arrangement is that the associate is assigned a section of the ministry and assumes the leadership of that section. If, for example, the associate is responsible for the Christian education (CE) division, the board may have delegated the supervision of that area to the Christian education subcommittee. If there is a subcommittee, the staff member who is responsible for Christian education will work directly with the CE committee. If there is no subcommittee, the staff member will work directly with the official board. Generally, though, it is a subcommittee rather than a board to which an associate might assume leadership.

A third type of relationship between the associate and the board and/or committee is that of an antagonist. The associate in this type of relationship sees the board or committee members as basically ignorant of the process or specifics of the ministry assigned to them. The associate sees as a major task the amending or correcting of any plans the board might make. The associate is the expert and insists on having things carried out in a certain way. This kind of relationship with the board or subcommittee tends to be argumentative and contentious.

The last kind of relationship is that of the associate as equal member with the board or committee members. Here the associate views the others on the board or committee as peers and as equally as competent as the associate. The associate tries not to assume more than equal responsibility for the tasks assigned to the board. The associate as equal member assumes no special privileges of rank or position. The equal-member associate attempts to fit into the existing group, but does not automatically assume any office.

There may be other types of relationships or combinations of these types of relationships, but these four give us a framework for a discussion of the basic issues. What are the benefits and drawbacks of each type of relationship? First, let's look at the benefits.

Benefits

A servant-type relationship benefits the board because the board controls the associate. When certain activities of the associate are evaluated against the ministry description, discrepancies can be noted. If it is agreed by the board that any aspect is ineffective or lacking in some way, corrective measures can be easily taken. If the associate has agreed to be servant to the board, the intervention of the board is not seen as intrusive but necessary and profitable.

A leader-type relationship benefits the associate because as leader of the board he or she has personal control of the direction of the ministry. The associate's assuming the leadership does not imply that his or her every idea or proposal will automatically be approved by the board or committee, but it does give the associate some control in the direction of the board's task. The agenda for the specific ministry can be regulated by the leader associate. An organization-type church will usually appreciate a leader-type associate.

Any benefit of the antagonist-type relationship might seem to have been eliminated by the nature of the relationship. How can the associate as antagonist have any possible benefit to the board or committee? The benefit for this type of relationship comes in the form of protagonist or provocateur. The associate was called to serve in a specific church because the perception was that the associate possessed certain skills that were needed. A benefit, therefore, may be the new ideas and challenges the associate brings to the board. The board may be tired of business as usual and appreciate the fresh perspectives initiated by the associate.

The equal-member relationship of the associate with the board benefits everyone because control of the direction of the ministry is shared equally. Here the organism-type church will appreciate an equal-member type of associate. The attitude here is that authority is shared, and it means that the paid staff does not have any more authority than the unpaid members of the board or committee. As an equal member, the associate, who is paid by the church, does not have more authority or responsibility than anyone else. This places the members of the board and other unpaid staff in the position of being able to make major policy changes and participate more fully in the ministry of the church. There are probably other benefits than these mentioned, but what about any possible drawbacks of each type of relationship?

Drawbacks

One drawback of the servant type of relationship is that the associate may feel that his personal ministry is demeaned. He may feel that all his preparation and experience has been put to little use if all he does is carry out someone else's plan or vision. Servanthood is not being someone else's lackey, but an associate who assumes this kind of relationship with a board or committee may begin to feel this way. Does not every associate want to make a significant contribution to his ministry assignment? Simply being obedient to the wishes of the board or committee may not fulfill the need for significance in the life of the servant associate and may in fact be a drawback.

The leader-type associate should certainly have his need met regarding a feeling of significance, but what about the followers? Some think that if a person is dominant and pushes a certain agenda that makes them a leader. A person with a specific vision and a demanding manner may not have anyone following. Board or committee members might be intimidated by the leader-type associate and withdraw support. Cooperation and enthusiasm may fade, and the leader associate may eventually find there are fewer and fewer followers to help in the actual ministry. It does little good to have the board or committee approve ideas if there are few to help accomplish the plans and execute the ideas. The leader-type associate may also create disagreements by being dogmatic and assertive with the board. This may be another reason for a possible lack of support for the leader associate.

The antagonist relationship of the associate with the board or committee can create an atmosphere of isolation for an associate. The ideas suggested by the associate may be creative and novel but that does not insure that enthusiasm for them will follow. It could be that so much antagonism has been generated in the presentation of the idea that people are reluctant to help. Battles fought and won in the planning stages may create hostilities and conflicts with others on the board. Hard-fought battles that are won may produce the feeling that the war is lost. Associates who assume the role of antagonist might receive a self-inflicted wound if they are too much of an adversary with the board. Challenging the status quo is good, unless it alienates the people who will implement the change.

The drawback most obvious to the equal-member type of relationship is a possible misunderstanding of the associate's role. Members of the board and/or committee have been assigned a role that has also been assigned to the associate. When the associate attempts to be an equal member of the board, other members may be confused. Some may think, *If the paid staff has the same responsibility as the rest of us, then why is the associate paid?* Another problem might be a conflict of interest related to the supervision of the associate. If the specific board or committee is responsible for the supervision and evaluation of a specific associate, how can that same associate serve on that same board? Is there not a conflict of interest?

Conflict of Interest

The problem of conflict of interest is not unique to the church, but certainly is present for many associates in the churches they serve. Take for example, the board or committee that interprets its task, at least in part, as the supervision of a certain associate. The servant-type associate would best fit into the board's perception of its task, and the other three types of relationships would fit less well. The predicament for the servant associate of feeling demeaned would certainly make any kind of evaluation of the associate's service more onerous to the associate.

The associate who assumes the role as leader of board or committee might be able to arrange an evaluation that reflects only the positive things and avoids the negative. The leader-role associate might want to avoid evaluation altogether and would be in a position to do so. This, of course, might conflict with the desires of the other members of the board. An evaluation might be necessary, but a strong leader-type associate may be able to block it or control it so no major changes would be necessary. Conflict of interest is certainly at its highest when the associate is the leader of the board that supervises the associate.

The antagonist associate may lobby for an evaluation, at least an evaluation of the program the board supervises. This type of request may be what the antagonist wants so that the changes desired can be more easily implemented. The request could, of course, backfire and do more damage than good. A conflict of interest could be low when the associate is antagonistic, but the situation could also easily become the board against the associate. The results could be negative for the associate if the role of antagonist is pursued.

The equal-member associate relationship, as mentioned above, might be very confusing for other members of the board or committee. How can one member of the group be singled out for evaluation? Will that member be excused while the evaluation is structured and/or implemented? How will the results of the evaluation be shared with the equal-member associate? What if there are difficult things to say to the associate? Who has the authority to say them, and who has the authority to enforce the implications of those difficult things? The possibility of conflict of interest is quite high with the equal-member associate.

These are only a few of the complications that can arise for the associate when it comes to conflict of interest. Each type of relationship with the board has different implications for conflict of interest. I suggest that each church and associate consider possible conflicts of interest when determining the type of leadership the associate should provide. Let's look now at the composition of the board.

Composition of the Board

Churches form boards or committees in various ways, depending on the polity of the church. For example, congregationally-run churches tend to *elect* their board and committee members, while elder-run churches tend to *appoint* their members. Some churches nominate a list of potential members, and the church affirms their appointment by vote. Some board or committee members may feel they are elected or appointed for life, in spite of what the church constitution or by-laws may say. They may feel that the area of ministry in which they serve is their ministry, and they feel a high level of commitment to it. Others may feel less of a commitment to the area of ministry and are serving on the board because of a sense of duty. There may be long-time church members or newcomers on the board. There may be people on the board who have nothing personally to do with the area of ministry they supervise. Other committees may be composed only of people who serve in that area of ministry.

Depending on how the board is composed, the focus of the work will shift. For example, a committee composed of workers in that ministry area will prefer to deal with operational issues. They will want to know what is being done about things such as materials and supplies, curriculum orders, and recruitment of needed workers. The board or committee that has no one on it who is directly involved in the ministry it supervises will likely care little for operations and normally will focus on policy. A combined board or committee (members of both types) will probably have a mixed agenda and perhaps be a bit more confused about its direction and purpose.

The associate who has chosen one of the relationship types discussed earlier will need to consider what type of board or committee it is they are called to work with. The type of board may affect the type of relationship they all need to have. For example, the leader-type associate will form agendas that will fulfill the purpose that the members of the board feel most deeply about. This will help to ensure a smoothly run operation as well as produce feelings of accomplishment and success. The equal-member associate will fit best with a committee composed of other involved workers. If the equal associate is the only involved worker on the board or committee, there will likely be a misunderstanding of the associate's role.

Individuality of the Associate

In spite of the composition of the board, the associate's role in relation to the board may be based more on personality than on anything else. For example, the associate who is a high *S* with the gift of helps would be perfectly content to fulfill the role of servant but would find it very difficult to assume the role of the leader. The associate with a high *D* and the gift of exhortation will find the role of servant difficult, if not impossible, to fulfill. There is no standard role for every associate with any given board or committee. Each associate will have to work out his role with the board as the situation becomes more obvious over time. Looking at some case studies will illustrate what I mean.

Case Study One

In one church I served, the senior pastor recruited a team of people to help organize and set policy for the CE program of the church. This ad-hoc group had no length of service attached but were to serve until the work was finished. I viewed myself as an equal member, and I called the group the Christian Education Leadership Team (CELT). I led the meetings, but was very open to everyone's ideas and suggestions. We set about our work by reviewing and accepting the goals of the CE program provided earlier by a general group. We then agreed to a leadership structure to carry out the goals. Various names were suggested to fill the posts. I noticed that there seemed to be some resistance on the part of the CELT members themselves to volunteer or to do the recruiting of the people whose names were mentioned. As minister of CE, I felt that if we were to proceed, I needed to shift my role and become more of a leader with CELT. I therefore volunteered to do the contacting of potential workers. Only one in the CELT group of about seven people expressed any interest in personally getting involved in teaching or leading. They were recruited to plan and set policy, and this service they were willing to do, but all except one were unwilling to step into a hands-on leadership role.

After the divisional coordinators and teachers for each of the classes were enlisted and had begun their service, the focus of CELT changed. The work of planning had been completed, and now the work of continuing supervision of the operations began. The meetings of CELT now had the divisional coordinators present, and the workers brought operational issues with them. The interest level of the original CELT members fell immediately. There was only one meeting after that where all the original CELT members and the new coordinators were together. In subsequent meetings, only one of the original CELT members and the departmental coordinators attended. Within a period of three or four months, almost all the members of the CELT group had been replaced and the focus had shifted from planning to operations.

I realized I was viewed by the CELT members as somewhat of an expert because of my position on the church staff, so the CELT members looked to me for direction and leadership. I at first approached my role with CELT as that of an equal member. I assumed that the church was organism oriented, so a leadership role would not have been appropriate. I did not want to take over and be a dictator, but I did have some ideas that I wanted to try to implement. I wanted CELT to catch the vision and get excited about carrying the vision to completion. I was hoping that each member of CELT would agree to take a part of the CE plan as their personal project and agree to serve as leader in it. When this did not happen, the purpose of CELT had to change. The members of the original CELT group no longer felt the need for their personal participation.

My role in CELT had to shift, also, but for other reasons. During the recruitment phase, I assumed the dual tasks of coordinator and lead teacher of one of the departments. By doing so, I began to feel the tension of being an equal member of CELT and being expected to be its leader. When the composition of CELT shifted from planners to workers, the policy-making function was more difficult to fulfill. Any evaluation of practice or change of policy could be construed to be a veiled criticism of the current workers. My volunteering to serve as a teacher of a class myself may have been appreciated by some, but one of the results was a shift in my relationship with CELT. Was I an equal member or its leader?

Case Study Two

In another church where I was an associate pastor, the CE committee was already in existence before I arrived. The church had elected a committee that served for one-year terms that could be extended indefinitely. Many had served on this committee for many years. The only officer they had was a chairman who was also a deacon and who also served as secretary. The senior pastor as well as the minister of youth and the minister of CE (me) attended all meetings of the CE committee. Agendas were compiled by the chairman alone, and the senior pastor had the final word on any decision. The committee was comprised of workers who each represented his or her specific ministry as well as members at large who had no specific responsibility in Christian education.

I found that my role with the CE committee was a bit muddled, both on my part and on the part of the committee. At first, I thought the committee expected the minister of youth and minister of CE to play the role of servant. The agendas were unknown to anyone except the chairman prior to the meeting. Decisions were made by the committee based on what the senior pastor wanted. Was the minister of CE expected to carry out the dictates of the CE committee? If so, I was not sure I was going to be happy doing what they decided. I wanted to influence the direction of the decision and to help shape the tasks I would be asked to do.

During the hour-long meeting, I tried to understand what was going on by observing the behavior of those present. I watched decisions being made, but was not sure who was responsible to actually fulfill them. It was obvious that I was not expected to be the leader of this group. The role of servant did not appeal to me as a long-term arrangement. The equal-member role might be what was expected, but it seemed to me that none of the other members were allowed to contribute anything of significance to the meeting. How could I be that kind of an equal member? The antagonist role would definitely not work because the senior pastor held the position of power in the committee. Taking the pastor on in front of the committee would certainly be a foolish tactic on my part. What was left for me to do?

I did not believe any of these three relationships would be workable for me or for the committee. I decided to try something. Without any prior approval by the senior pastor or chairman, I rashly suggested that I be given some leadership in the group. I suggested that I consult with the senior pastor and the chairman and create an agenda for the group. It was a bold move on my part, since I had been in the church for only two weeks. This was my first meeting with this group, but as a result of the suggestion I was granted a form of leadership. I was now able to shift my role from servant, antagonist, or equal member to more of a leader in this group. The group responded positively to my suggestion. They accepted me in this new role and showed their support by participating fully. Over a period of five years, there was no turnover of membership. There was not one CE committee member who was even absent from a monthly meeting, except a single member who was excused due to an out-of-town business trip once every three months. I was allowed to serve as a leader associate for the tasks assigned to the CE committee. I also found personal fulfillment in providing direction to a CE program that served to meet the needs of the church. It proved to be a mutually satisfying relationship that lasted a long time.

Conclusion

The associate's role with the official board or ministry-area committee is a crucial one. Depending on which type of relationship is chosen, the associate can be happy in it or be terribly frustrated. It makes sense to try to choose a role that suits the associate's individual temperament and meets the needs of the church. Being perceived as a leader will depend on the specific church's expectation for the role of the associate and the associate's ability to play that role. After all, the conductor and the player must be in complete synchronization in order for beautiful music to pour forth.

Discussion Questions

Use these questions privately or in a group, such as a church staff, to apply the points made in this chapter.

1. In what way does the official board of your church receive applause or boos for the work of the staff?

2. How does the official board of your church interpret the ministry of the associates to the church as a whole?

3. Which, if any, of the four types of relationships of an associate to the church board do you mostly follow (servant, leader, antagonist, or equal member)? What makes you answer as you did?

4. Does the church board have a clear idea of the type of role they expect associates to play in your church (servant, leader, antagonist, equal member, or other)? Is it the same for all associates?

5. Do the associates in your church have a clear idea of the type of role they expect to play with the church board? Is there a difference between the answer for number three and number four? What can be done about it?

6. Are you or the other associates in your church happy with the relationship the board expects you to perform? Explain why.

7. Other than those given in the chapter, can you think of other

benefits of an associate's fulfilling each of the types of relationship with the church board?

8. Other than those given in the chapter, can you think of other drawbacks of an associate's fulfilling each of the types of relationship with the church board?

9. Is one type of relationship of an associate with the board more biblical than another? Support your answer.

10. Is there a conflict of interest in your relationship with the board? If yes, what is the nature of the conflict? How is the conflict related to the type of relationship expected or actually played?

11. What is the composition of your board or committee—planners (noninvolved in the actual ministry) or practitioners (involved in leadership of groups they supervise)?

12. Is your board composed of long-timers or short-timers in the church? If both, is there a balance, or more of one than the other? What difference does length of time in the church make to the way the task of supervision is carried out by the board?

13. What part does your individuality play in the relationship you have assumed with your board or committee? Does your personality support the relationship the board expects to form with you?

14. If you could make a change in your relationship with your board or committee, what would it be?

CHAPTER TEN

How Should I Play with Those from Other Orchestras?
(Outside Fellowships)

Members of a local orchestra or ensemble sometimes have the opportunity to play with musicians of other orchestras. There may be a city-wide gathering for an all-community concert or there may be smaller groupings of players. These special times allow the musician to hear other players and compare notes with them. These larger groupings of musicians may provide a new kind of outreach to the communities involved and extend the influence of each orchestra. Playing with other orchestras is viewed by most musicians as a chance to stretch one's skills and find inspiration for one's own music. Such times can be a real highlight of the musician's life.

Not unlike the musician, the associate will have opportunities to interact with those in other ministries. Associates may find others in similar vocational positions outside their local church ministry or meet with pastoral staff from other ministries. These types of opportunities will be discussed in two ways, the first being church-to-church fellowships and the second being individual fellowship.

Church-to-Church Fellowships

Churches that are part of a denominational fellowship will be expected to participate in programs for the churches in a given area. Denominations go by the name of fellowships, associations, movements, or some other name, and they are grouped together and called denominations even though they may refer to themselves under a different name. If there is a national or regional office for the denomination, that office usually takes the lead in cooperative ventures. Programs can be centered around a certain ministry function, such as evangelism or training. "World Wide Communion Sunday" was such a program for which I received annual materials from the denominational office. Materials are produced for each local church to use for programs the denomination wants to promote. Sometimes the materials are simply sent to the church without the church's ordering them. Other times, the church is required to purchase the special materials for the special program. It can become difficult for the local church to decide whether to participate. Churches have to decide if they will use the many different programs coming from the denominational office in addition to programs from other sources.

Another way church-to-church fellowships are encouraged by denominational leaders is through cooperative meetings. Denominational meetings can be citywide, regional, national, or international. Some church groups elect representatives to go to these meetings on behalf of the individual church. Usually, the larger the group, the more formal the meeting. In national meetings, resolutions are passed and decisions made that may affect every church in the association. Meetings of a lesser scope than national often meet for training, evangelism, worship, or some similar purpose.

Churches not in a denomination can find many local and regional meetings for their church's participation. The independent church can be every bit as busy with outside meetings as the denominational churches. It all depends on the initiative taken by the leadership of each church. There are meetings in every major city for men, women, Sunday school teachers, worship leaders, church administrators, and so forth. Pastors whose churches are not affiliated with a denomination and yet are interested in cooperative ventures, will find ways to collaborate. Those who are not interested in cooperative ventures will find reasons to refuse.

Church Politics

Often in church-to-church involvement there is a political nature to the activities. Cooperation with the denominational program or participation in regional activities take on political dimensions similar to what happens in the local church. The decision to order the materials and participate in the denominational program is certainly as political as it is programmatic. Staff members ask, How will our church be perceived if we do not fully participate with this program or in this particular meeting? Does nonparticipation with such activities reflect on the leadership of the church, and the church as a whole? The answer is definitely yes. The political fallout of nonparticipation as well as participation must be assessed.

Once the fallout has been assessed, one must deal with the political nature of the meetings themselves. Combined church meetings tend to exhibit self-promotion and one-upmanship. Church A (or its pastoral staff) sharing with others tends to be interpreted that Church A is somehow better than the rest. Why would they be selected to share if they were not doing something special? How can those who are sharing not help feeling special—a notch above the rest? Even outsiders brought in to speak have some uncommon characteristic about them or their ministry; otherwise, they would not be invited to speak. Large group meetings can fall into the trap of comparing themselves with others and bragging under the guise of sharing. A pecking order develops among the churches and that makes some feel low on the list.

The church that feels especially put down, ignored, and not called on to share is the smaller church and its pastoral staff. Usually the larger church or the staff member of the larger church is called on to speak, not the small-church leader. The cult of the bigger and better swells as everyone present understands why certain churches are looked to for leadership and others are routinely ignored.

How would an associate feel if he and his church are overlooked in these cooperative fellowships? The associate would probably feel no different than the ignored pastor or the ignored small church. The difference is, the associate will normally be a part of a larger church because it is usually a larger church in which an associate serves. Since the associate has the advantage of being in a larger church, any competition is between the associate's and other larger churches. In this sense, the stakes are higher for the associate. This competition can be just as fierce as with individual associates on a single local-church staff. Associates can use the larger group to jockey for higher positions or for recognition. Of course, these activities are couched in terms of sharing for the benefit of others.

Pressure to Conform

Churches that are affiliated with a denominational fellowship will probably experience greater pressures to conform than those that are not affiliated. Programs are sent from the denominational office with the expectation that each church will cooperate fully. Denominational officials know that not every church will, but if a large proportion of the churches do not, the program or meeting cannot be effectively completed. Denominations need to feel useful to the churches they oversee.

Some churches may decide to partially participate in a particular program or meeting. The degree to which each church cooperates with the program of the larger group is usually decided by the staff of the church, though other churches can use the denominational program as a type of pressure on individual churches, and some denominational officials might appeal personally to a church to participate. The pressure is greatest on the largest churches. If the largest of the churches participate, then the others will likely follow.

The appeal for participation might even be personal if the denominational leader happens to know the church leader personally. All pastoral staff know that it is not likely that perks such as appointments to prominent denominational committees will be given to the nonparticipants in denominational programs or activities.

The pressure on the church associate to participate in a denominational program can be intense. If it is determined that it would be politically unwise to decline, the associate must select the elements of the program or meeting that will be utilized. I know how difficult it is to use only part of a program because many of the parts are interrelated to each other, with one part built on another. If all the parts are not used, then it becomes apparent that the program cannot be fully accomplished and the purpose adequately achieved. It may prove to be very difficult to use only a portion of the denominational program and have it fit into the program of the local church without too much disruption. The desire to be viewed as a strong supporter of the denomination increases the pressure on the church leaders to conform.

It is possible that the very large church that has ignored the denominational programs or activities can become isolated. Isolation does not seem to concern the large church as long as it continues to grow and be successful. Denominations, however, do not like the largest church becoming isolated. It may become necessary for the denomination to try to incorporate the large church back into the fellowship, which may be done by inviting their pastors to speak before regional or national meetings. This may or may not work. Sometimes these large churches have enough clout to cause the denominational office to change its program and adopt the program of the large church. It has happened that some of the largest churches simply feel no value in being associated with the denomination; thus they withdraw.

International Connections

Another type of church-to-church relationship is that of an American church with one from another country. The churches that initiate the search for such a relationship with American churches are usually from underdeveloped countries and want the help the American church can provide. In such cases, it is next to impossible for the American church to avoid a kind of paternalism toward the other church. The church in the United States may think it has so much more to offer the church from another country. After all, the American church will probably have a beautiful building, a large congregation and staff of ministers, and a big budget.

From my own experience, I have found that the church from the other country may have much to teach the American church. For example, the very things that we think are effective and successful are missing in the Baptist churches of Latvia. Effective ministry is happening there, not because of the outward trappings of church life but because of the commitment of the people. After fifty years of Communist rule, the Latvians are taking back the control of their country, and the church of Jesus Christ is strong and vibrant. If only the churches of America could possess the spiritual depth of the Latvian Baptists, we would learn more than we could possibly give to them. We would certainly drop our paternalistic attitude toward churches from other countries.

As with other types of church-to-church cooperation, it is necessary for the local church of America to evaluate the motives for international cooperation. Displaying what Americans think of as success in church life or effectiveness of church programs may not fit the needs of the other church. Issues of cultural difference and insensitivity may reduce the benefit received by both churches. Displaying how much better we are than they can only lead to disappointment with the international church-to-church experience.

Competition

Competition with other churches is probably the biggest problem an associate encounters when cooperating with outside organizations. One of the first questions associates ask each other at any fellowship time after the preliminaries is, "So, how is your attendance?" "What are you doing that is really effective?" This is translated to mean, What programs are bringing in more attendance? Quality is often associated with size, and the church with the largest attendance is somehow perceived as the best. Associates who serve in the largest churches are given special privileges because it is thought the associate had something to do with the large attendance. The attendance of the church program the associate is in charge of may have little to do with his or her church skills and abilities. Competition should have no place in our church lives, but the reality is we usually relate to other churches as rivals more than as colleagues.

Perceiving our colleagues as rivals does more harm than our pitting one group against another. It is also harmful when competition causes a rupture in relationships between individual ministers.

Individual Fellowships

If the church is part of a denominational fellowship, there will be regular meetings of the pastors and usually the full-time church-staff members. If the church is independent, there are still many ministerial fellowships that are available. There is hardly a day that passes without an announcement about another imminent seminar, workshop, or conference. Ministerial staff can travel within their respective cities, to regional meetings, or to national conferences. There are often interdenominational conferences for staff members who specialize in a certain ministry, such as youth or children's ministry. Not being in the same denomination is no hindrance to fellowship with others in a similar ministry; the fellowship is simply of a different kind.

The kinds of meeting can vary from fellowship over a meal, to prayer for each other's needs, to seminar training, guest lecturers, sharing of ideas that work, and so forth. These times will certainly include fellowship, no matter what the focus of the time spent together may be. In fact, fellowship seems to be the most important element in these types of meetings. How can the fellowship at these meetings become meaningful to each associate? How can *koinonia* take place between associates from different ministries?

The associate, as any person in ministry, realizes that he or she has a unique opportunity to share in the lives of others. Things may be said in confidence that must not be shared with anyone else. There are some with whom you would never share anything from your own life because you know that it would be on the grapevine or in the rumor mill before nightfall. You may have been burned by gossip and backbiting before, and you do not want that to happen again. What are you going to do? There are, however, certain things that each associate needs to share with someone else. Who will that person be and how can the fellowship be meaningful?

Intimate Fellowship

An associate will have a closer relationship with some members of the church than with others. There may even be a special person or small group with whom a confidential relationship may develop. You find yourself being able to tell them anything and know it will go no further. You are able to vent your frustrations and the others become a "sounding board" for your ideas. To use David Smith's term, they become intimate friends.

The associate who is married may feel he or she has a built-in confidant. This is true, but the nature of some confidences may preclude telling your spouse what you may need to say. In fact, telling one's spouse may not be appropriate if breaking a confidence is involved. If a confidence is not involved, telling a spouse the burdens of your heart may be entirely appropriate and appreciated by both the spouse and the associate. Ask yourself, Would telling my spouse what is bothering me unnecessarily burden him or her? I am not

134

advocating the keeping of secrets between married partners, only suggesting caution that sharing with the spouse should not compound the problem. If the spouse is part of the problem, he or she should be spoken to directly, not spoken about to someone else. An associate may need a person outside the situation to help give clarity and be a channel of the wisdom of God. A spouse may be too close to the situation to give objective help.

Many associates have fallen morally by sharing a personal problem with a member of the opposite sex. The situation may start out innocently enough, but soon it gets out of hand. For example, a male associate may share with a female that his spouse is inadequate, does not meet his needs, and so forth. The female tries to comfort him, and the intimacy moves to psychological and perhaps to physical intimacy. Many associates have destroyed their lives and the lives of others in this fashion. I feel it is important to share on a deep level, but limit such sharing to those of your own sex. Problems may still develop, but the likelihood of moral failure is less.

Guidelines for Intimacy

Being vulnerable with another person is important, but there are some guidelines for establishing an intimate relationship. The first, which has already been mentioned, is to select your partner from the same sex. This will reduce the risk of difficulty further on in the relationship. Fellowships between two couples do not seem to provide the kind of intimacy that is created between two of the same sex. Doing things as couples can be useful, but it is not necessary that the spouses develop the same kind of relationship that the associates enjoy. In fact, it may be that the associates' fellowship does not include the spouses at all. It should not be assumed that because the associates meet together that the spouses should do the same. That would be entirely up to each set of spouses to decide.

A second guideline is to discuss the regulations by which you will live. For example, will there be a regular meeting time and place? What will be the length of that meeting time? What about food? What will be considered confidential and what will not? Are some topics off-limits? If so, what are they? Knowing the regulations eliminates potential misunderstandings. The limits can, of course, be renegotiated as time passes and needs change.

An important third guideline for the associate to remember is the perceived status of the participants. If, for example, an associate with little practical experience and who is newly arrived in the church is paired with a mature, experienced senior pastor from another church, the latter naturally assumes the superior, and the former the inferior, position. The experienced senior pastor may feel that there would be little personal gain from such a relationship, and thus he rejects the relationship. Two associates of the same sex who share similar responsibilities in similar-sized churches and have comparable education and experience would feel less difference in status. Those with a comparable status would be more likely to make their sharing useful to both.

A fourth guideline is, evaluate the quality of sharing. For example, if one associate is unwilling to share anything personal, the other should have the freedom to call attention to the difference in depth of sharing. Perhaps some rules need to be added or current rules changed. If the relationship is satisfactory to one and not the other, straightforward and frank discussion is the only way to rectify the situation. To make this kind of discussion easier, have preset evaluations at periodic intervals. That way, one person does not take offense when the other suggests the necessity of evaluation; it is simply the preplanned activity agreed upon.

A fifth guideline is to limit the size of the group. The kind of intimacy that is shared should not be disseminated to a large group. A maximum of five or six persons is a manageable size. A minimum of only one other is necessary, but the upward limit should not be above six. There needs to be a sense of connection established among the members of the group, and a large number of participants reduces the likelihood that all members will be engaged in similar ministries. The larger the city, the greater the pool from which an associate can draw. In a small city or town, there may be only one other who shares the kind of ministry that you do. There may be no one with whom you can share. What if there is no one who fits the narrow confines of your particular kind of ministry?

If you find yourself in that situation, the final guideline has to do with your reaching out to someone who has no direct connection with you vocationally. This might be a Christian who works in a secular setting but has a similar task, such as a Christian music director from the local high school or college. A principal from a local elementary or secondary school might have enough in common with an associate who serves as minister of Christian education for intimacy to work well. A retired minister who lives close by could be a splendid resource and prayer partner for an associate. One such person was a rich source of support for me at one time in my life.

How to Get Started

After the connection between associates has been made, they need to determine together the purpose of their meeting. If one associate takes the initiative and invites several others to meet to discuss the possibility of such a group, the purpose may have been stated. For example, if the purpose is accountability, some may feel uncomfortable with that purpose and decline the invitation. If the purpose is stated as fellowship, perhaps fewer would decline. Be careful that you don't use the bait-and-switch system and say the purpose is fellowship and then later switch the purpose to accountability. Be upfront about what you think the purpose should be, based on your own needs. If others share your needs, they will want to join. If they do not, they can decline at the outset and avoid misunderstandings later.

Once the purpose is established, the rules and regulations by which the group will function will be easier to formulate. If the purpose is personal accountability, the rules will differ dramatically from those of a meeting where the purpose is fellowship. Any set of regulations or rules needs to have some type of consequence if the particular regulation is not fulfilled. If you have, for example, a standing appointment every month, and one or more members feel free to miss it without informing the others, what should be done? Attendance becomes especially important when the group is small. It's a waste of time if only one person shows up and the others do not come or send a message. Frustration and disappointment with the way members of the group treat one another will not insure a meaningful and worthwhile association. These things need to be understood in the beginning of the relationship.

If the purpose of the group is accountability, members can begin by sharing what it is they want to be held accountable for. Members of the group should avoid the temptation of pointing out what others should be doing or becoming. It is true that most members will start out by sharing something that is innocuous, impersonal, or relatively unimportant. This is usually done to test the resolve of the other members of the group. If the unimportant issue is handled well, the person sharing will probably move to deeper levels and more important issues. Over time, the level of sharing can become very meaningful and important to the individual and to the group.

Deep-level sharing takes time to develop, and close relationships will not be immediately noticeable to all involved. The larger the group, the more difficult it will be to have an intimate relationship with everyone involved. If the group only numbers three, there will be at least six distinct relationships in it. If a group has six, then the number of relationships is thirty. It is unrealistic for anyone to expect all thirty relationships to be developing into intimacy at an equal rate. Jesus had his three special ones within the twelve disciples.

Conclusion

Fellowship with other orchestras and other musicians can be a profitable and meaningful experience for the musician. The associate can find value in meeting with others in both church-to-church and individual relationships. If care is taken, some of the pitfalls can be avoided and some of the benefits will become obvious to those who desire quality in this kind of fellowship. The effort required to reach out to others is well worth it.

Discussion Questions

Use these questions privately or in a group, such as a church staff, to apply the points made in this chapter.

1. Do you find your church pressured in any way to participate in church-to-church activities or programs?

2. Does your church generally participate in whatever the denominational office sends to you? If yes, do you feel as though you must participate, or are you free to decline? On what does your declination depend?

3. If your church is not in a denomination, is your church generally known as a participant in church-to-church programs or activities? If yes, what reasons can you give for your participation?

4. Are the church-to-church meetings or activities as political as this chapter claims them to be? Why or why not?

5. What kind of political fallout have you experienced because you did not participate in some church-to-church activity or program?

6. What kind of political fallout have you experienced because you *did* participate in a church-to-church activity or program?

7. Have there been elements of competition or one-upmanship in church-to-church activities you have observed? If yes, what are they?

8. Have you or your ministry in church-to-church meetings been ignored?

9. Have you seen denominational perks, such as an important committee appointment, given to those who usually do not participate in denominational activities?

10. Does your church have any kind of international church-to-church connection? If yes, has it been profitable for both? In what way(s)?

11. Do you have any individual or small-group fellowship you could call intimate? If yes, how has it helped you? If no, do you feel the need to find one?

12. How do you feel about same-sex intimate fellowship versus coed? What about couple fellowships? Have you found them to work in developing intimacy?

13. Does your fellowship have written or unwritten regulations by which you function? Do you sense any need for revision?

14. How would you evaluate the status of each member of your group? Are you all equal, or does someone have a higher status? How does the status of the members affect the level of intimacy in the group?

15. Do you share personal things in your group or are you stuck at the superficial level?

16. Is there any evaluation built into your group? If yes, is it proving useful? If no, how could you incorporate evaluation?

17. Does your group number six or less? Have you found the kind of intimacy you desire from a larger or smaller group?

18. Are there associates in your area who have a ministry comparable to yours? If the answer is no, what can you do about finding someone with whom to share fellowship?

19. If you need a group that holds you accountable, what specifically do you need to be held accountable for?

20. Are you satisfied with the progress your group is making toward intimacy, or do you despair you will ever arrive at that destination? If so, what can be done about it?

Part 4:

Lessons from the Trenches

CHAPTER ELEVEN

How Should I Prepare for Performance?
(Organizing for Success)

Orchestras must be organized in order to be successful. Musicians need people who make sure the music is ready, the music stands and lights are in place and working, the chairs are arranged, and the podium properly positioned. If the orchestra is on the road, there are the logistic issues of transporting everybody, their luggage, their instruments, and all the rest of the necessary equipment. Someone is needed to organize the orchestra, or the concert may never happen. Beautiful music is only possible if the orchestra is organized.

Associate pastors find themselves in a similar situation to that of the orchestra in that their work must be organized in order for their ministry to be effective. Since the work of the associate is frequently self-originated, and mostly self-governed, it is important that the associate know how to manage well. Haphazard activities will bring no lasting results.

Rather than discussing special designs for specific types of ministries, I will examine a general approach to ministry that will fit most associates. Then I will illustrate the principles with two case studies from my own experience. But first, where does organizing fit into the management of the work of the church staff?

Leadership

In any ministry, there must be a leader. This leader normally plays the role of a visionary who sets the direction of the ministry. This visionary is often the senior pastor, who, in cooperation with the official church board, attempts to determine and promote the vision to the congregation. The senior pastor takes the lead and holds the banner high so all can see and follow it. The direction of the church may be a specific emphasis, theme, or focus for the ministry. It is best when everyone, including every member of the church staff, gives full cooperation to the fulfillment of that vision.

Any ministry also needs managers, or those whose responsibility it is to carry out the particular vision chosen by the church. The associate staff are often viewed as managers because they are assigned prescribed duties within that overall vision. The visionary says: "We are at point A, and we are going to move to point B." The visionary may not feel obligated to know all of the steps that will be required to move the church to point B. It is the primary role of the staff managers to create ways and means to see that the church does in fact move from A to B. Associates are often measured by senior pastors, official board members, and the church in general according to the ability to manage the part of the vision assigned to them.

Management

A classic example of how management actually occurs are the five sequential functions described by R. Alex Mackenzie. The five functions of management are planning, organizing, staffing, directing, and controlling.[1]

Planning

The first function of management is planning. Some may ask, "Should associates make plans for their work?" "Why not just trust the Lord?" Does not Scripture say, "Many are the plans in a man's heart, but it is the LORD's purpose that prevails" (Prov. 19:21)? I do not believe this verse implies that men should make no plans at all but rather should depend on God when making plans. The associate who manages well will make plans, but throughout the process, there must be sensitivity to the will of God. Not trusting God and making your own plans is working in the power of the flesh. God's work will not experience God's blessing if done in the strength of the flesh.

Making plans that express God's will requires intentionality. If there is no plan of action, the associate will not be effective. The old adage says that "if you fail to plan, you plan to fail." Refusing to plan might be an expression of laziness or an unwillingness to change. Associates need to have an intentional plan and then proceed to work that plan. Failing to plan cannot be blamed on not knowing God's will, for God has given us sufficient direction through his Word, the Bible.

Planning should not be a solitary activity. Also in Proverbs it says, "plans fail for lack of counsel" (15:22) and "make plans by seeking advice" (20:18). The staff, paid and unpaid, must be taken into the associate's confidence when plans are made. It is helpful to seek advice from those outside the church as well. It is wise to consult with those other staff, because they will be needed to carry out the plans.

It is wise also because others can provide assistance to brainstorm ideas that are creative and unfamiliar to the associate.

Mackenzie says the first step in planning is forecasting, but the future is based on an evaluation of the present. The associate must assess the current situation, therefore ongoing program activities should be the first evaluated. Programs include personnel and curriculum. Careful preparation of all of the areas to be evaluated and the means to evaluate them is important. Bias can often be seen in the type of questions asked, so be sure you know the purpose for seeking each facet of information. Try to make any inquiry as brief as possible; people's time is valuable.[2] Facts should be gathered and the problems analyzed. Setting a course of action should not be attempted until a thorough job of evaluation is done.

After evaluation, the next step is forecasting what the present course of action will likely produce. Is there, for example, a downward trend in participation, from the unpaid staff as well as the church constituents? What results would this downward trend produce in the future? Has the number of unpaid staff or visitors been increasing, decreasing, or staying the same? What effect would this kind of outreach have on future plans? How is the morale of the staff? Is there excitement and joy in their service for the Lord, or is there only complaining and bickering? What will be the probable outcome if things continue as they are?

You may say that you have never been good at predicting the future. Nor have I, but it is not necessary to be able to predict unknown events that are totally out of the context of your ministry. It does not take a clairvoyant to see what will likely happen if current trends in your ministry persist. Trends can be turned around of course, but if nothing is done about the current state of affairs, the outlines of the future can be seen, even if the details cannot.

Objectives can now be set based on the difference between what is and what could or should be. Determining the desired outcomes is akin to a dream in that some things may be desired in your ministry that have little basis in the current reality. These objectives may be corrections of the problems or novel activities or programs that have never been tried before.

Mackenzie refers to the term *objectives* in his chart, but goals and purposes must be set before objectives can be determined. The whole church should be involved in the formulation of the mission or purpose statement of the organization. The role of the senior pastor is to serve as a leader in rallying the church around a central purpose that is memorable and clear. Every member of the church staff should wholeheartedly support the mission or purpose statement.

Goals for the church's mission statement can be determined by a smaller group such as the leadership team of the church. These goals are subheadings of the central purpose and often are related to the divisions of labor among the church staff. For example, the minister of evangelism might be responsible for setting and carrying out the goals that relate to evangelism. Goals should be measured periodically, usually each year. Goals are normally the device used to evaluate the effectiveness of the staff member.

Objectives are specific outcomes that relate to specific goals. Objectives often are attached to certain church programs, so it makes sense that the workers in that program set their own objectives. Programs are designed to reach specific short-term objectives. Objectives cannot be set indiscriminately and are necessarily tied to a specific goal and the overall mission or purpose of the church. Objectives are often short-term, usually three to six months in duration. Objectives are very specific and precisely measurable.[3]

Another element of planning includes developing strategies of how and when to achieve goals and objectives. To program means to establish the priority, sequence, and timing of the steps necessary to achieve the outcome. Resources are allocated, procedures are standardized, and policies are developed. Strategies will be adjusted later as the program develops, but these initial steps are necessary for the planning stage.

Organizing

Organizing is one step in the management process, but it is often the name given to the whole, as in this chapter's title. Organizing, according to Mackenzie, is only a part of the whole management process and begins with the establishment of an organizational chart. The chart helps to delineate the relationships among all those involved in the management process. Descriptions of the positions on the chart, with responsibilities and authority, are completed. Determining the qualifications of each person to fill each position is also required.

Using the terms discussed in chapter 8, it is the organizational model, rather than the organism model that is being utilized by Mackenzie. If the organizational model is followed in your church, then his model will have some merit for you. If your church is more organism oriented, then you will need to modify his procedures of management. For example, certain elements, such as planning, would originate with the unpaid staff rather than with the paid staff. In effect, each unpaid staff member would become a manager of ministry. A more complete discussion of organization and organism as a basis for church ministry is found in chapter 8.

Staffing

Mackenzie's next step logically flows from the previous ones. Now is the time to recruit qualified unpaid staff for each position in the organization. The new people are familiarized with the situation and trained to be proficient through instruction and practice. Unpaid staff are not abandoned to do their work as soon as they are placed, but are continuously helped to improve their knowledge, attitudes, and skills. Here the equipping ministry of the associate comes to the forefront. I have discussed recruitment in more detail in chapter 8, so I won't repeat it here.

Directing

The next function in the management process is called directing. The associate delegates responsibilities to the unpaid staff, who have exact accountability. The unpaid staff is helped to take the desired and required actions through the associate's inspiring management. Motivation is increased by discovering what is specifically meaningful to each worker.[4] The associate manages the staff well by coordinating the efforts of all. Developing a team of workers that functions smoothly is important to the success of each team.

When each worker and each team is given the responsibility for a distinct area, conflicts inevitably arise. The associate should take the initiative to help resolve the conflicts that develop. Placing the trust for the details of the program with the workers themselves stimulates creativity and innovation in the achievement of goals. Change is never easy, but any innovations will be easier if those who will make the changes are the ones who thought of them. If the associate brings the changes to the staff, the ideas have to be sold to the workers before they have enough enthusiasm to carry them out.

Controlling

The final function in the sequence of Mackenzie's model is controlling. The term sounds heavy handed and aversive, but it need not be. Controlling in this context means the establishment of a reporting system for the critical data that is needed as well as how and when it will be gathered. Performance standards constitute the conditions that should exist when key duties are well done. Without the standards, it is impossible to measure results. Measuring results is indispensable to ascertaining the extent of deviation from the goals and standards. When it is necessary to take corrective action, plans and procedures are adjusted accordingly. When no correction is required, various kinds of rewards are in order.

Management Style

The key to effective management in ministry is the cooperation of all who are involved in the process. Bernard Bass has supplied a massive compendium covering all the major literature on leadership. He gives ten categories of theories about leadership.[5] It is impossible to review all of these here, but the category that seems to have the most relevance to the church is called the humanistic theories.

Hersey and Blanchard's "Life Cycle Theory of Leadership" (1969, 1972) is a theory of leadership effectiveness synthesizing Blake and Moulton's (1964) managerial grid postulations, Reddin's (1977) 3–D Effectiveness typology, and Argyris's (1964) Maturity-Immaturity theory.[6] Leader behavior is related to the maturity of subordinates. As subordinates' maturity increases, leader behavior should be characterized by decreased emphasis on task structuring and increased emphasis on consideration. As maturity continues to increase, there should be an eventual decrease in consideration. Maturity is defined in terms of subordinates' experience, achievement motivation, and willingness and ability to accept responsibility.[7]

The associate who develops a fixed type of managerial style will find it difficult to have a successful ministry over a long period of time. Ability to read the landscape and to flex so as to meet the needs of the particular situation is essential for effectiveness. No certain managerial style should be thought of as fixed for eternity. One key to effective leadership is a high degree of cooperation by all the workers involved.

A good management style is one that helps every unpaid staff member feel like a member of the ministry team. The associate will need to determine if his or her preferred leadership style contributes to the cooperation of the ministry team or hinders it. Adjustments can be made if the associate knows what kind of style is needed to become an effective manager of ministry teams. When implementing any of the functions of management discussed above, an associate who invites and listens to input from a wide group of unpaid staff will find the most effectiveness in ministry.

Two Case Studies

I would like to describe for you how Mackenzie's five functions have been applied in two specific situations. These examples are my own, but I will refer to them as Church A and Church B to retain anonymity. The situations are similar in that they both deal with youth ministry, and I was the paid staff in both. The situations were not separated by time by more than two years, but the two churches were separated by 2500 miles or so. They existed in two different cultural settings; one was a small town (approximately 30,000 population) and the other a suburb of a large city (approximately 1 million population).

Church A had a senior pastor who was very supportive of my ministry. Church B was between senior pastors at that time. In both situations, I was responsible for Christian education as well as youth. The number of unpaid staff in both churches was low. I had been in Church A for about three years, and I was in my first year in Church B. The size of Church A was about 580 and Church B about 700.

Church A

The Youth for Christ Club (YFC) in our small town met in our church on Tuesday morning at 7:00 A.M. The largest group of students in the club came from our church. The director of the YFC club in our town had grown up in our church, and his entire family attended regularly. The youth president of the club was a member of both our church youth group and our church. Church A was highly invested with both people and financial support in the ministry of the local YFC.

It became obvious that the youth from Church A felt YFC was more meaningful to them than their church. Leaders from among the youth were hard to enlist for the youth group, and when activities conflicted, YFC was chosen over the church youth activity. The YFC choir was a popular organization, and all of the church youth wanted to be in it. Cooperation between the two youth ministries was almost nil. Each conducted its own program but did so for some of the same youth. Any collaboration between our church and YFC seemed to be unnecessary and unwanted by the director of the club.

I evaluated the situation with the senior pastor, and we concluded that a change was needed. If both programs were to continue, competition and rivalry would be the result. I decided that the goal of ministry to the youth of the town should not suffer because two ministries could not cooperate. My goal was to integrate the two ministries into one seamless one. I developed several strategies that included singing and playing in a folk group that performed at the YFC rallies. Another strategy was to fully participate with YFC in an evangelistic outreach during an annual festival held by the town. I volunteered to take charge of the training of the counselors. These youth were identified by their responding positively to the survey that was used at the festival.

I set the procedures and policies for the counselor training, always careful to work within the guidelines set by YFC. The line of authority was such that I worked under the director and took responsibility for a specific task. I set the qualifications for counselors and began to recruit those who were needed. I led several training sessions to prepare them to counsel at the festival. Various counselors were assigned to cover each of the nights of the festival. I was present each night at the festival to answer any questions, to provide the materials the counselors needed, and, in general, to encourage them in their ministry. The few conflicts were handled easily because I was able to make a decision on the spot. Counselors developed their own styles as they gained experience, and I tried to help them work with youth who fit their style.

The reporting system was arranged by YFC in advance, so it was just a matter of carrying out the procedures. Follow-up was arranged with various churches for youth who either were from those churches or had expressed a preference. Those youth who were not from a church or who expressed no preference were divided among the churches that supported the event for follow-up. Results were easily measured by counting the number of those who received Christ each night. Any adjustments were made as needed, but as I recall, all went smoothly and as planned. Counselors were thanked after the festival concluded, but their reward was primarily the joy of seeing many come to Christ as their personal Savior.

Church B

Church B was located in an affluent suburb of a large city. The youth from that church expressed little interest in the activities I planned for them because they desired more excitement than games and a hot-dog roast at a local park. Events that required much planning and expense were preferred. I sensed a spiritual lethargy in the youth that mirrored the adults' spiritual lethargy. If the current situation were to continue, I saw myself cast into the role of party pastor for the youth group. Arranging social events was not what I thought my total ministry should be. There had to be a change.

I set some goals and objectives that related to the needs, as I saw them, of the youth group. I wanted to reach out to the unsaved youth while at the same time incorporating the church youth into the excitement of evangelism. I designed a weekend called "YouthQuake"[8] that incorporated several major activities, including a banquet one night, a VW race the next, and special activities on Sunday. We invited a special speaker who was to speak at the banquet and in the morning services on Sunday. The budget for the weekend was greater than any youth activity the church had ever had before.

The YouthQuake weekend was proposed to the board of trustees, who held the purse strings. The board balked at the proposal mainly due to the expense of the weekend. They reasoned that since the proposed activity was not in the budget, it could not be approved.

There was no extra money to cover such a large youth event. The board suggested that the youth pay some of the expense by charging for the events. They also thought other activities could be held before YouthQuake to raise money to help cover the expenses.

These suggestions by the board seemed reasonable enough, but the dates for the event that were preferred precluded scheduling any money-raising activities beforehand. The idea of charging the youth an admission fee for the events was carried out. The result was that the board cut the proposal drastically and allowed only a fraction of the total amount requested.

I was serving as head of YouthQuake and there was no committee that helped me plan it. Since there was no senior pastor, there was no counsel available to me from that source. I asked various people to assist, but I did not know who possessed certain skills that might have been helpful. I just asked those I knew. There were no position descriptions or qualifications for the positions. There was no training provided as I simply depended on each one to carry out the task that was assigned. I did not do much to motivate those who agreed to work. I do not think those I asked knew who the other workers were; we did not meet together as a group.

All coordination was done by myself, and I remember frantically running about trying to confirm that all last minute details were completed. There were conflicts, such as some workers not completing assignments as I had hoped. Those tasks had to be left undone or alternative options performed at the last minute. There were some complaints about the food at the banquet or about the cost of the events. It seemed I had the whole weekend as my responsibility and when something went wrong, I received the blame. I don't remember anyone who thanked me for the work involved in YouthQuake. For that matter, I can't recall anyone who received Christ as Savior or who told me of being ministered to in any way. Some said, however, that they had fun at the VW race. The program had to be pared back in significant ways and was less of a major event and less effective than I had planned it to be.

Evaluation of Case Studies

Using the five sequential functions as described by Mackenzie to evaluate the two events helps to show more clearly what happened. The planning phase of Church A was done in concert with others, whereas Church B was not. The need for the plan was not conclusive in Church B, but in Church A it was. Establishing a need basis is crucial to gaining the support needed from others to make the plan work effectively. Everyone in town knew what the festival was and how it ran. Explaining our part in the festival was easy to do for Church A. Church B had no idea what a YouthQuake was or why it was needed.

The role of the senior pastor was crucial in each situation. Since there was no counsel from a senior pastor in Church B, the likelihood of success of a major event could have been predicted. The counsel of the board of trustees was not followed. I charged ahead into disaster. Church A had the wise counsel of the senior pastor, and my decisions were guided by him.

The organization phase of the Church A event reflected the structure of YFC, as I placed myself under the authority of that ministry. The line of responsibility was clear to me and the task was understood. The Church B situation was less clear as far as responsibility was concerned. I felt the responsibility to do something to turn around the youth program, but enlisting others to help me was difficult. It had not been widely established that YouthQuake was the best vehicle to accomplish what I thought should be accomplished. I failed to take the time necessary to organize a team or work group to help me carry out whatever plan was devised. I tried to carry the burden alone.

The directing phase of the management process in Church A was easy because the task and relationships were understood by the workers and myself. Church B had no such understanding. The burden of coordination, motivation, and conflict management was assumed by one person—me. This burden was too great to bear.

By the time the management process arrived at controlling, the Church B situation was careening wildly out of control. Since no performance standards had been constructed, it was impossible to objectively measure if those who had been delegated responsibility had done it. I measured it subjectively by my own idea of what should have been done, but the people who helped me had no clue. It is no surprise that I was disappointed with the results. Church A revealed that few corrective measures had to be taken, as those recruited carried out their responsibilities as expected.

On the whole, the situations differed in result because of the time that was available to plan. Church A took plenty of time, whereas Church B rushed the event needlessly. Another reason the results differed was the amount of time I had been in each church: Church A was year three, while Church B was year one. It is crucial to understand the context in which the ministry occurs, and in Church B there was insufficient time, so the understanding was not there.

Conclusion

Understanding the management process is a significant factor in the associate's effectiveness in ministry. Just as in an orchestra, someone has to understand what needs to be done and know how to achieve it. The role of the associate as manager is a vital part of productive and useful ministry to the church.

Discussion Questions

Use these questions privately or in a group, such as a church staff, to apply the points made in this chapter.

1. Is the distinction between visionary and manager helpful to you? Does it apply to your church staff? How?

2. Of the five functions given by Mackenzie, which is the most important to your ministry? Why?

3. Of the five functions given by Mackenzie, to which do you give the most attention? The least? Why?

4. What are some of the reasons you fail to plan as you should?

5. What part of planning is the most trouble—evaluation, forecasting, or goal/objectives? Explain.

6. Does your church function more as an organization or organism? If both, what elements can you identify for each type?

7. To what extent do you equip your unpaid staff for their ministry? Give specific examples.

8. Do the members of your unpaid staff have exact accountability for their ministry or are they left on their own?

9. What can you do to increase the accountability of your unpaid staff?

10. Do you have a means to regularly evaluate the ministry of your unpaid staff? If yes, what? If not, what should be done about it?

11. Is your management style flexible enough to shift from task structuring to consideration when your group indicates that is needed? What evidence can you cite?

12. Have you ever had an experience similar to Church A in the case study? How about Church B? What were they? What did you learn from your experiences?

How Do I Perform at Home?
(Modeling Faith to Children)

The individual member of the orchestra plays an instrument within a group of people with whom they have chosen to associate. This group may be friendly, and warm relationships may develop, but this group of performers, in a technical sense, is not a family. The members of the orchestra may be a proxy for the orchestra member's family but not actual family. When the rehearsals and concerts are over, the instrument is packed away, and the orchestra member goes home, what kind of a person greets the family? Is there a noticeable difference between the public performer and the private family member? Is the performance affected by the private life of the performer?

When it comes to ministry, the family plays an important role in the associate's life. The marital state of the associate has been discussed in chapters 1 and 2, so the emphasis here will be on the role model the associate provides for the family, especially the children. A minister is to "manage his own family" (1 Tim. 3:5), and the role model presented is a vital part of that management. If the associate has a personal life that contradicts the public life, what will the effect be in the family? If the associate has an exemplary family life, matching what Scripture says it should be, will this support and strengthen the associate's ministry? These questions will be answered, but first, a little theory will be helpful in understanding how the associate fulfills the function of modeling in and for the family.

Role Model Types
A helpful contribution to understanding modeling has been supplied by the social theory of Albert Bandura.[1] He posits that a major function of modeling is to transmit information to observers, and such information can be conveyed through physical behavioral demonstration (direct), verbal description, or pictorial representation (symbolic).[2] He claims these are different kinds of modeling that have certain applications. Learning in young children depends extensively on the direct behavior modeling of others because children imitate the behaviors of others. As linguistic competence is developed, verbal

modeling (description) often substitutes for, or supplements, behavioral modeling as the preferred mode of guidance. Verbal modeling can convey with words an almost infinite variety of behaviors that may be too inconvenient or time-consuming to portray behaviorally.

The last type of modeling Bandura calls symbolic. This is where social learning at any age is influenced through some form of media, such as books, still pictures, films, television, and other forms of visual media. This last type of modeling expands the scope of influence from one's immediate community to diverse sources from everywhere and anyone. Research has found that children and adults acquire attitudes, thought patterns, emotional bents, and new styles of conduct through symbolic modeling.[3] Unlike learning by doing, which requires shaping the actions through repeated trial-and-error experiences, in symbolic learning a single model can transmit new ways of thinking and behaving to many people simultaneously in widely dispersed locales. The more people's images of reality depend on the media's symbolic environment, the greater media's social impact.[4]

Modeling of the Associate

Behavior modeling on the associate's part is observed by a wide variety of persons, not just the family members. The associate's behavioral modeling will of course be scrutinized by spouse, children, other family members, and close friends. Neighbors, acquaintances, and every member of the church being served will also observe. The associate's life is on display for all to see. It is the family, however, that has the best view of the match between the associate's private behavior and the associate's public behavior. It is the family that can affirm or deny the integrity of the associate.

It is common knowledge that when children are small, the associate, as any parent, will probably be seen by the child as perfect and capable of all things. Even the mundane task done by the parent seems miraculous to the small child. There comes a point in middle to late childhood, however, when the parent is no longer idealized and becomes a real parent. Children recognize that their parents are unable to accomplish the miraculous. What are the dynamics of that shift? What causes the shift and can these causes be predicted? What is involved in this process and how does it affect the developing religious faith of the child? Is the shift away from parent inevitable? Is a rejection of the parent's religious faith by the child inevitable? By the age of eighteen, will the child have chosen to follow Christ or gone the way of folly? Will my children confirm or deny the conclusions they have made about how well I have modeled my religious faith?

These are questions every Christian parent wants answers to, and they will now be addressed.

Hypocrisy

Jesus told his disciples about "the yeast of the Pharisees, which is hypocrisy. There is nothing concealed that will not be disclosed, or hidden that will not be made known" (Luke 12:1b–2). I am not sure that our Lord had the family in mind when He said this, but it surely applies. I believe that hypocrisy is the biggest issue that parents face with their children in the teen years to adulthood. Children need to know on many fronts if their parents are hypocrites or the genuine article. When it comes to faith, children test their parents to see if they live up to what they say they believe. Do the private decisions of the family match the public pronouncements at church? Children will often accept the faith of their parents willingly if parental faith is authentic. The issue of hypocrisy is compounded when the parent is a minister of the Gospel. Children of ministers assume the existence of some type of parental faith and find it is central to who and what the family is and does. The place of personal faith is prominently displayed by the minister as something very important and becomes very clear to the child early in life. How can a minister urge others to trust Christ when one's own children have rejected it? Assuming the age of accountability is below age five for normal children, how can an unbelieving older child be explained? If the associate cannot be successful with the children in his own family, how can he expect to be successful with others? Is there something about the associate's personal life that is blocking his children from believing?

It is interesting that the professions regulated by ethics (medicine, teaching, and counseling, to name a few) seldom exercise constraints on violators as strictly as they do on ministers. A surgeon whose children do not possess the same values about medicine, for example, is not restrained by the AMA from practicing medicine. A counselor whose family life is a mess is generally not restrained by the state from practicing. Teachers often have difficulties at home but continue to teach in our public schools. But if a minister's children do not accept Christian values, the minister may find he is unable to continue an effective ministry.

It is as if the associate's vocational life, no matter how effective it may be, is discounted if his children fail to accept the public teachings of the associate. The primary work of associates is evaluated by secondary means, in this case, the lives of their children. Many ministers have found themselves in trouble because of the reaction of others to the problems of the minister's children. Perhaps it is not fair, but it seems the minister's children are held to a higher standard than are the children of other professionals and even to a higher standard than the children of any other members of the church.

Hypocrisy may not be at all related to a minister's children rejecting the faith. Every child is an individual and develops his or her own set of assumptions about life. But it is well-known that early childhood studies confirm that the child's first few years of life are a foundation for all later development.[5] Depending on one's theological stance, children may be a part of the covenant parents have accepted.[6] Whether or not children are thought of as part of the covenant family of God early in life, the impact of the parent is the most important one for the child's religious development. Why would children not desire to follow the faith of their parents if they concluded that parental faith was genuine and authentic? There are some important principles involved in the process of rearing a child in the faith.

Child Training

Scripture says, "Train a child in the way he should go, and when he is old he will not turn from it" (Prov. 22:6). The Hebrew word for "to train" is *hanak* and means to dedicate to God, and "the way he should go" means the proper way, the path of wise, godly living. The phrase "when he is old" refers to when the child is grown to adulthood. The result is "he will not turn from it." This result is not always guaranteed, as there are conditions, which are stated by other parts of the Proverbs. Throughout Proverbs, beginning with the first seven verses, children are urged to shun the way of folly and choose the way of wisdom. Children may choose the way of folly because of self-will or deliberate disobedience. For that choice, the child is held responsible. *The Bible Knowledge Commentary* says: "It is generally true, however, that most children who are brought up in Christian homes, under the influence of godly parents who teach and live God's standards (cf. Eph. 6:4) follow that training."[7]

Socialization Process

The process of training a child in the way he should go is one of socialization. Every person grows up receiving many kinds of social influence. It is the role of the parent to help the child evaluate influences and reject those that are not leading them toward godliness. Parents should not overprotect or smother their children but help them to wisely choose the right path. The selection of friends and activities are vital to training a child in the way he should go.

I will summarize some of these steps in the socialization process of children. These steps can be employed to guide a child to affirm faith in Jesus Christ and in the values of the Christian parent. Each step will be described in a sequential manner, beginning with the infant. You may be an associate who is a young parent and inexperienced in the skills necessary to train children. You may be older and have passed through these stages with your children. Whatever your stage in life, you should be able to compare your personal experience with the descriptions that follow. If you find yourself seriously deficient in child-raising skills, as I did when I started out, you will discover some help here. It is crucial to be able to raise your child in the nurture and admonition of the Lord.

Infancy

A Christian parent can never begin too early. As soon as the child is born, the Christian parent can begin being a godly influence.[8] Singing songs to the child about God, praying with and for the child, reading Bible stories, and taking the child to church can begin the process. By placing objects in the home, such as religious art or plaques that can be explained to the child even before the child speaks, you establish a pattern of godliness for the child. Playing Christian music in the home is a good way to influence the child. The manner of the parent with the infant is also important. Treating the child with love and tenderness and in a caring fashion reflects the love of our heavenly Father.

Toddler Age

Once the child begins to talk, there will be many questions, and the parent has the opportunity to patiently answer them. Assuming the existence of God, the parent establishes the nature of God on the child's level of understanding. For example, a child can learn that God loves and cares for us and that we should thank Him. A child learns by imitation of the parent, so prayer times as a family will teach that speaking to God is as natural as speaking to anyone. Bible stories with pictures and reading to the child can create a special time. Christian children's music can communicate important spiritual truth. The church nursery can reinforce what is learned at home with loving teachers and a curriculum designed for the child's age.

Kindergarten

The child who begins kindergarten enters a much bigger world than home or church. Other children in the Christian-education class can provide an opportunity for the child to implement what has been learned. For example, hearing that it is a good thing to share with others can be mere words for the child until experiences in the classroom reinforce the verbal message. Social groups, including the parents, can contradict or reinforce the teaching the child receives.

God is becoming more real to the child as imagination is separated from truth. For example, children will be confronted with the figure of Santa Claus. Is he a real person? If parents do not distinguish between real and imaginary people, the child is apt to be confused when confronted with contradictory information.

Once we took our children to the toy department in a large downtown store at Christmastime. We got off the elevator on the floor where the toys were, and we were greeted with a long line of parents and their children. They were all waiting to see Santa. As each child arrived at the front of the line, he or she was escorted into a room where the next available Santa was located. There were eight different rooms with eight different Santas. The children were escorted so that they supposedly would not see the multiple Santas. We were not sure our children saw that there was more than one Santa, but we were not afraid of being "caught." We had informed our children that Santa was an imaginary person and part of a little game that adults played with children at Christmastime. My wife and I talked about the situation later, and we wondered what the other children were thinking if they saw more than one Santa. We wondered how the parents would explain this ludicrous situation to their children.

This story illustrates the importance of being honest with your children about what is imaginary and what is not. If the child finds out later that Santa was a hoax, it would be easy to question the existence of other noncorporeal persons, such as God. Be clear that Santa is not real, but God is.

Primary Age

The primary-aged child, grades one through three, will normally be very trusting toward the parent and most adults. Children of this age should be encouraged to place their trust in God for every aspect of their lives. The world of the child is expanding and Christian parents can expose their children to a wide variety of experiences. Day trips to museums, parks, and other activities will help children learn how God relates to their broader world. Trusting God when trouble comes, such as when the child might be lost or the car breaks down, can provide memories that center on God's provision.

In our family we involved our children in our ministry in various ways. There were plays, musicals, and outreach events such as five-day clubs and vacation Bible school. They were not forced to take a leadership role, such as a part in a play, but they could if they so desired. We shared with our children the joy of serving Jesus.

Keeping your word to a child is important, for the primary-aged child has invested much trust in the parent. To break a promise, no matter how insignificant it may seem to the parent, can be a major source of disillusionment to the child. If a parent can violate a promise, the child can generalize that broken promise to other things. How can anyone be trusted? Can God be trusted to keep his word?

Later Childhood

The child of grades four through six will begin to ask the hard questions, so parents should expect them. Some questions may be about evolution and the creation story or about how people can be saved who have never heard the Gospel. Some may ask why, if God is loving, is there so much pain and suffering in the world? Parents should not panic but patiently answer the child as best they can. If the parent has no answer, begin a research project together to find it. Above all, be honest with the child if there is no answer. Being straightforward with a child will mean more than thorough answers. If you don't know, tell the child so.

The underlying issue for a child of this age is the trustworthiness of Christianity. The child begins to ask, "Was all that I have been taught from childhood the truth or an elaborate deception?" "Is following Christianity something I want to do personally or should I follow it because it has been expected?" It is during this age that children begin to evaluate the quality of their parents' Christian role models for authenticity. The verbal descriptions of Christianity by the parent must match the direct behavioral observation by the child.

It is likely (very likely) that the parent will disappoint the child in some aspect of living the Christian life. What should a parent do in this situation? It is easy to assume that the mistake was not noticed by the children and ignore it. If it is obvious that the parental *faux pas* was noticed by the children, to ignore it is disaster. The child knows that you blew it, you know that you did, but you fail to acknowledge it, and the child could easily think that you are a hypocrite or so dense that you do not even know that you blew it.

The only way out of this dilemma is to confess to your children that you know what you did is wrong and ask for their forgiveness. You as a role model are at stake here, so it is vital that you affirm what the children already know. Confessing your sins to your children does more than affirm your honesty. Confessing your sins sends the message loud and clear to your children that perfection is not possible in them or in your life. In fact, confessing says that perfection is not expected. That is a great relief to a child.

Early Adolescence

Early adolescence, grades seven through nine, is a period of role confusion and the formation of identity.[9] Young people are being confronted with the heaviest peer pressure of their short lives. The drive to become their own persons and individuate from their parents can center on the religious question. The decision to follow Christ or not will normally be affirmed during adolescence. If the child received Christ as a young child, new questions may be raised about the validity of that decision. If the child has never taken a personal stand for Christ, the pressure will be great at this age to settle the matter.

It is no surprise that many children raised in a Christian home receive Christ during childhood and adolescence. It is also no surprise that reevaluation of that decision usually occurs in early or middle adolescence. Doubts about the faith are to be expected from children, and wise parents will use the doubts as springboards to continue the discussion about the value of personal faith. The faith of a child will be tested during adolescence. Will it emerge as gold or be destroyed by the fire? Parents can help their adolescents explore the possible results of rejecting the Christian faith. Will the parent still express love to the child if he or she refuses to follow Christ and the faith of the parents? Early adolescents must feel a sense of security during this time of life.

Adolescence

When children arrive at grades ten through twelve, they are nearly adults, at least as far as the age of majority is concerned. An eighteen-year-old expects to be given adult responsibilities and, in some ways, be treated as an adult. If it has not been settled before, it is during adolescence that the decision about following Christ becomes crucial. In some ways, it is now or never. Impending adulthood brings a seriousness about this decision that was not sensed before.

An important issue is how the associate will handle the possibility that his or her child might reject the faith. It is certain that the minister remembers the passage of Scripture that asks, "If a man does not know how to manage his own family, how can he take care of the church of God?" (1 Tim. 3:5 NASB). There may be great parental guilt stemming from this verse. This verse may also be used by the parent to bludgeon the child with guilt, by pointing out to the child that the parent's continuation in the vocational ministry may depend on the child's making the right faith choices. It very well may be true that the associate's ministry might be affected by the behaviors of his or her children, but the parent's pointing this out might be interpreted as coercion.

Any form of coercion by the parent might backfire and provide the adolescent with more reasons to reject the faith of the parents. It is probably better to help the child discover some possible results of rejecting the faith. This way, the child is able to make a more intelligent decision of his or her own free will. Any decision for Christ made under coercion will likely be repudiated at a later time anyway. It should be pointed out that delaying a decision is really an untenable situation. Sitting on the fence about one's faith can be very uncomfortable, and a decision one way or the other will bring a welcome sense of resolution.

What if the decision is to reject the Christian faith and live a life apart from God? What if the child makes a freely chosen decision that is the exact opposite of what the parent desired? Can the associate allow his or her child the freedom to decide against Christ, knowing that it may destroy the associate's ministry? To do this would probably break the hearts of the parents and send them into a depressing tailspin of guilt and remorse. If parents genuinely desire that their children make their own decisions about the faith, independently and without duress, then the decision to reject must be accepted as a possibility. Parents pray that their children will not reject the faith, but experience shows us that they need to be ready in case it happens.

If, after all the training and prayers by the parents and the church, a child does choose to reject Christ, the child must be released to live the life he or she has chosen. Parents should remember that the child's life is not over and should continue to pray and to reach out in Christian love. By all means, do not reject the child because he or she has rejected Christ. The child may be administering another test to the parents. The child may be asking, Will you love me if I do not love your God, your Jesus? The verse in Proverbs says "and when he is old he will not turn from it" (22:6). A child may still come back to God. Never give up hope that God will touch the child in a deep and life-changing way. He or she may need to experience some serious trouble before seeing a personal need for God. Parents need to be there for the child when he or she is going through these difficult times.

When to Resign

When is it appropriate for associates to recognize that it is time to resign because of their children's behavior and values? There are many steps that precede the associate's resignation. This is the subject of the next chapter, but I will discuss this issue now from the standpoint of family.

Let's assume the question of resignation has been precipitated by some event or series of events in the family. The rejection of the Christian faith by a child of an associate minister will likely reveal itself by later childhood. Let's also assume that all efforts have been made to determine if there are extenuating circumstances that have caused the child to act out. Tests may reveal there may be a learning disability, for example, that affects behavior in Sunday school but has little to do with the child's faith. All possibilities of mental or physical causes should be eliminated.

Parents will have noticed any negative attitudes of their child, and any associated behaviors that need correction. Other adults, such as Sunday school teachers or church leaders, might notice and share a concern with you about your child. Generally this is done by others in a spirit of helpfulness and not criticism. Corrections should have been made all along but may reach a critical point in childhood. Minister parents should not panic, but discuss with the child what is causing the negative attitude and disruptive behavior. If good communication has been practiced between parent and child, the problem may be resolved at that level.

If the discussion with the child is not fruitful, that is, no change is evident, then additional steps must be taken. A professional counselor who specializes in the problems of children should be consulted. There may be additional tests the counselor may wish to conduct to help in the diagnosis. Having a child who is in therapy is not a reason for a minister to resign, anymore than if the child was hospitalized for a physical illness. It is entirely appropriate for the associate to apprise the senior pastor and the church leaders of the situation and to ask for prayer.

If the child does not respond to the therapy over a period of time, he or she will carry these problems into adolescence. Adolescents are capable of doing more harm to themselves and their parents because, being older, they have more resources at their disposal. They may have a job, which provides money and a bit of independence, an automobile, and friends who may not be appropriate. The potential for difficulty is exponentially greater in adolescence than in childhood.

Often, during the high school years, a series of escapades and misadventures lead to the major crisis of a child's life. Dropping out of school, drunkenness or drugs, an unwanted pregnancy, a conviction for a crime, or some such problem may be that crisis. It seems that it is now time for the associate to seek the counsel of the senior pastor and other leaders of the church.

Telling the leaders about the associate's wayward child may be very difficult but necessary. All questions should be answered and wise counsel sought from the pastor and church board. Since the associate serves the church, express to the leaders that you want to do what is right for your child as well as what is right for the church. Tell them you will do what they decide. You submit to their leadership in this matter as in other areas of ministry.

The church board may commiserate with the associate and recognize that the problem child is no different from others in the church. Other leaders may have had similar problems with their own children. They may make suggestions about what can be done or how they can help. They can choose to be supportive during this crisis. They may suggest that the associate take some time off, or some type of help may be provided.

The board may decide that the associate can no longer minister effectively until this problem is resolved. It might be suggested that the associate take some leave time to focus on the family problem. This period may or may not be with pay, but without pay it seems to only add to the problem by reducing the family income at this time of trouble. There may be a structured plan of recovery established for the associate's family. This is an intermediate step and the associate should still not resign. Staying in a place where help can be found is wiser than moving to another place where everyone and everything is unfamiliar. The help the associate needs is found in the church, among people who know the situation.

The board may, however, simply request a resignation from the associate. They realize effective ministry cannot proceed and decide to eliminate the problem. The resignation may be effective immediately or at some later time. When the church requests a resignation, the associate has no other alternative but to comply.

The board's decision to ask for resignation may not be based entirely on the home situation. There may be another reason for the board to ask for resignation, and the crisis with the child may be a convenient excuse. It seems that if the associate's ministry is appreciated and the church leaders do not want to see a departure, more will be done to try and restore the associate and the family. If the associate has other problems or is seriously ineffective in ministry, the board can avoid confronting the issues and accept the home life of the associate as inadequate. The result is the same, but the blame is shifted from the official board to the associate who failed "to manage his household well."

Some associates refuse to accept the counsel of the official board and try to appeal to the church. Coalitions are sometimes built among the associate's friends against the board that has called for the resignation. When the coalition lobbies for the associate, a major church fight usually occurs. The result of such fights is that the associate still leaves the church, and many of the coalition leave also. It seldom seems wise to cause a church split over this kind of issue. The associate should listen to the counsel of the pastor and the board of the church.

Conclusion

The associate's family life is vital to his or her effectiveness in ministry. It is true there are higher standards for ministers than other church members, but the stakes are higher also. The life of the associate affects many others inside and outside the church, so every associate should take care to insure that he or she, and also his or her children, honors Jesus Christ. There is hardly a greater joy than seeing your own children grow up in the nurture and admonition of the Lord.

Discussion Questions

Use these questions privately or in a group, such as a church staff, to apply the points made in this chapter.

1. What aspects of your life and ministry might be called symbolic modeling?

2. Is the single associate relieved of responsibility for his or her model of Christian faith? How does the modeling of the single associate affect his or her family?

3. When did the shift from the idealized parent to the real parent take place in your child or children?

4. Is hypocrisy among Christian parents as big a problem as this chapter makes of it? Why or why not?

5. Can you supply names of any associate ministers who have been barred from ministry because of a failure of their children to live the Christian life?

6. What would you like to add to the socialization process described for each age level in this chapter?

7. Do you make it a practice to apologize to your children when you fail in some way? If no, why not? If yes, what have been the results?

8. Do you expect perfection out of your children? What makes you answer no? What makes you answer yes?

9. Have you ever used the guilt trip as a tool to force your children into making the right faith choices? If yes, what were the results?

10. Are you able to affirm your child's ability to make a free decision about his or her faith, without coercion from you? Why or why not?

11. Why would a board choose to ask for resignation rather than restoration of the associate? Are there reasons other than blame shifting?

12. Have you ever seen a coalition that lobbied for an associate against a church board to be effective? Explain.

13. Do you think the submissive response to the board's counsel is the wisest move for an associate? Why or why not?

CHAPTER THIRTEEN

How Do I Move On to Another Orchestra?
(Terminating Gracefully)

There comes a time when the player in an orchestra feels the need to resign. A performer may retire, become a solo artist, move to another orchestra, or get out of music altogether. What are the factors that would cause a musician to decide to leave the work for which he or she has trained and has been doing for so long? What are the issues that are involved in termination, and how can it be done gracefully?

Associates sometimes find themselves in situations such as George's. Having accepted an associate position in a new church only nine months before, George thought he had done enough investigation beforehand. He was reasonably assured that everything would go smoothly in the new ministry. There were little things that happened in the first nine months, but George ignored them as routine and unimportant. Then something happened that made him think that he could not ignore things anymore.

George had heard some complaints about the ministry of the adult department, mainly the Sunday school classes. He heard that the teachers were not very good and that the material was boring and irrelevant to life. Sunday school attendance for the adult classes was declining. The adult fellowship groups that were held in homes were far more interesting to adults than Sunday school was. Some asked, "Why does the church need both programs?"

Since this area of ministry was George's responsibility, he felt the criticism personally. He wondered if his future ministry was threatened along with the adult ministry. There were so many repeating the criticisms now that George felt that something had to be done. But what? And if something was changed, would it be enough to quell the criticism? Would the changes save his ministry in that church or would the situation get so bad that he would have to leave?

I will first address the issue of termination by discussing why an associate should not leave the ministry. I will also supply a response for each of the issues mentioned. Then, I will discuss reasons why an associate should consider resigning. But first, to further introduce the subject, I will discuss two items—the type of resignation and length of service or tenure.

Type of Resignation

The associate might encounter the question of termination, but the reasons for it might be rather benign. For example, an associate might be retiring and leaving church ministry. There may be health reasons for the associate's resignation. Another church may call and inquire if there is any interest in the associate's moving to their church. These are always flattering contacts, but it does not mean the associate need say yes to every inquiry. These are relatively benign reasons to submit a resignation, and the senior pastor, official board, and church usually accept these with regret but without much fuss.

Another type of resignation is one done under pressure. This type of resignation has a more abrasive edge to it, and hard feelings may result. Reasons for resignation under pressure might include conflicts or unresolvable difficulties that may lead to the church's asking for the associate to resign. Resignation under pressure might not even disclose to the church the real reason for departure.

An associate needs to know when enough is enough. How does the associate know the difference between a minor skirmish or a major battle? When should the associate dig in and fight, and when should the associate give up and start looking elsewhere? How much should be told to the senior pastor, the church board, or the church at large? Should the associate try to bargain for better conditions? Should the associate resign with no other position and wait on the Lord? When is the best time to resign? Should the associate "tell the whole story" to the whole church in a final farewell? Can burned bridges be crossed again? Does length of service make a difference? These are some of the issues that will be discussed in the following pages.

Long Tenure

Let me say at the outset that I think long tenures of service by associates are very good. Long tenure speaks volumes about the associate. It says, for one thing, that the associate has good interpersonal skills and is able to work out the conflicts that inevitably arise. While some associates move every three or four years to a new ministry, the advantages of a long tenure over a short tenure are many. If the associate has a long-term plan, the results of that plan may never be experienced if there is a move every three years or so. Frequent moves disrupt the family, especially when the children are in elementary and secondary school. It is common that the length of stay of most associates is shorter than that of senior pastors. I believe tenures are so short because church staff people find it easier to flee than stay and try to work out the conflicts. What are some insufficient reasons for an associate to move on?

Reason Not to Leave: Criticism

An associate might be discouraged by criticism. The cause for the criticism might have been a poorly planned and executed event or program. The associate may be bored with the repetitiveness of the duties or the lack of support from the unpaid staff. Discouragement might be due to fatigue or an undiagnosed illness. Whatever the reason, the criticism is often interpreted as, You are incompetent in your responsibilities!

There is an old story that helps us understand an important fact about criticism. An old man was riding a donkey, and his son was walking behind. Some criticized the father by saying he wasn't fair to the son. The father agreed, so the boy rode and the father walked. Further down the road others criticized the boy for not giving preference to his older father and allowing him to ride. The son agreed, so both the father and the son rode the donkey. Further down the road, others criticized both of them for violating animal rights. So both got off the donkey and all of them walked. Still others criticized them for being so stupid and letting a perfectly good ride go to waste.

The moral of the story is, If you want to avoid criticism, do nothing. Of course, that will not work either, because then you'll be condemned for being lazy. Criticism comes to everyone who does something, and it seems to be unavoidable. If you allow what someone else says to discourage or disappoint you, you will do nothing. Focus on the positive in people's lives that results from events, activities, and programs.

If comparison with others is the basis for criticism, remember what Paul told the church at Corinth: "'But let him who boasts boast in the Lord.' For it is not the one who commends himself who is approved, but the one whom the Lord commends" (2 Cor. 10:17–18). Comparing your ministry to someone else's is foolish. Believe what God has said about you and ignore the rest. Criticism in and of itself is not a good reason to resign.

Reason Not to Leave: Interpersonal Conflict

Some associates claim that criticism cannot be ignored because some people in the ministry are impossible to get along with. There may be an unpaid staff member who always has an opinion contrary to yours. The interpersonal conflict may be with the senior pastor. Nothing an associate does may be good enough for him, or the associate's plans are trashed before he or she has a chance to implement them. The official board may be divided as far as the associate is concerned. Some are supportive, and some make comments about a wide variety of concerns from many outside sources. At the core of all of these issues is the interpersonal relationship on which cooperative ministry is based. The interpersonal dimension of the ministry is extremely important.

With any two people, it should be expected that there will be varying points of view on ministry issues. Differing viewpoints, however, doesn't mean there must be conflicts between the parties. As said before, the associate needs to take the initiative in the resolution of these conflicts. Taking an intransigent stand about unimportant issues with those who supervise you is imprudent. Know what an important issue is and where to take a stand. Some of those important issues will be discussed in the next section of this chapter. But interpersonal conflicts per se should not require an associate to resign.

A basis given for conflict is commonly referred to as "a difference in philosophy of ministry." This euphemism probably refers to the methods chosen for ministry practice in a specific church. Practices of ministry are always based on some assumption, such as a doctrinal belief or set of beliefs. If the doctrine is agreeable to the associate, then it may be the application that is not. An associate should have become aware of the methods used by a church before agreeing to the call. Everything ever done in the church cannot be known in advance, but the general methods used by the church in the past should not be a surprise to the associate. But what if the associate finds new methods or suggests novel approaches for the church that are deemed to be incompatible with what has been done in the past?

I am assuming that a high level of communication exists among the members of the pastoral staff. Senior pastors and their associates should be able to discuss together new ideas and what the implications would be for each of the various areas of ministry. A high level of openness and frankness should characterize these discussions. If this type of communication is happening regularly, how can philosophical differences drive a wedge between the members of the pastoral staff? Perhaps it would be more accurate to say that the reason an associate is leaving is because there was poor communication.

What price has to be paid for good communication to occur? The sacrifice of a certain amount of ego is necessary for good communication. It takes time to communicate well and that will have to be carved out of one's schedule. A high degree of openness among the pastoral staff is needed. An agreement to support one another in and out of the official meetings is required. An associate who makes disparaging remarks about his senior pastor behind his back will find the desired kind of communication to be lacking. Learning how to communicate well with every member of the church staff will eliminate interpersonal conflict as an adequate basis for resignation.

Reason Not to Leave: Family Issues

Another reason to say no to resignation would be issues that relate to the family. Since we discussed children as a reason for resignation in the previous chapter, we will not do so here. There are other family issues that might present themselves as a basis for possible resignation, such as illness or injury or personal health problems. Are family issues such as these an adequate basis for resignation?

I say no because the church can be a wonderful support for the associate when family illness or injury occurs. It is the body of Christ that can provide the care and sustenance that is essential during the time of trial for the associate. Any member of the church can expect a degree of care during illness or injury. Why should the associate feel he or she should be treated differently?

The issue may be related to continued financial support, however. If the associate is unable to work, shall the church continue salary and benefits? How long will salary and benefits be continued? Most churches should, but few do, carry disability insurance on associates, nor do most associates carry such insurance themselves. If the church terminates an associate just when financial support is needed, the associate and family are placed in a very difficult situation.

If the associate feels he or she must resign to relieve the church of the financial burden placed on them by the illness or injury, it is best to let the church determine this. If there is long-term disability involved, the church will need to make some kind of arrangement to fulfill the responsibilities of the associate. In addition, a plan for recuperation and restoration of the associate must be made in order to achieve the best interests of all involved. Thus, I don't think a short-term illness or injury should cause the associate to resign. In the case of long-term disability, the church leaders can make the best decision for the associate and for the church.

Reason Not to Leave: Broken Promises

Some associates may claim that there have been broken promises either from the senior pastor or the official board. Promises made during the interview period to the associate may or may not be kept. Promises made to me during one such candidating period were not kept. I found that the search committee gave answers to my questions that sounded reasonable to them. Unfortunately, the official church board was not consulted and had different answers than the search committee. Were promises broken? The answer depends on your point of view. From my point of view as an associate it seemed that promises were broken. From the view of the official board, nothing was promised to begin with, so no promises were broken.

Broken promises may seem to be an appropriate basis for resignation, but are they? Peter asked Christ, "How many times shall I forgive my brother when he sins against me?" Jesus answered, "I tell you, not seven times, but seventy-seven times" (Matt. 18:21–22). Jesus was not commanding a specific number of times we are to forgive but was illustrating the unlimited magnitude of our forgiveness. We are told by Christ, "For if you forgive men when they sin against you, your heavenly Father will also forgive you. But if you do not forgive men their sins, your Father will not forgive your sins" (Matt. 6:14–15). Are broken promises something that cannot be forgiven? I believe broken promises are an insufficient cause for the resignation of an associate.

Are there any reasons that may be legitimate for saying yes to the question of resignation? Let us turn to a few that might be sufficient cause.

Reason to Leave: Heresy
The first cause that would qualify as a basis for resignation is doctrinal deviation. Differences of opinion about doctrinal issues will certainly exist on a church staff among the pastors. But is that doctrinal deviation heresy? Every church will have a statement of faith and this is a good place to begin. If the difference is not explicitly stated in the statement of faith, is it significant enough to cause the associate to resign? How will the associate know the doctrinal positions of the other members of the church staff before accepting the call to come?

The associate who assumes unanimity about doctrine on the church staff may find surprising differences. The differences in doctrine may be acceptable to the associate and the staff, or they may not. Charismatic gifts, such as speaking in tongues, may be allowed in public services, or they may not. Would this make a difference to the associate one way or the other?

The differences in doctrine may seem to be objective, but they are subjectively chosen. What may seem crucial to one may not be important at all to another. One associate may refuse to stay at a church that believes in infant baptism, and to another that practice and belief seem insignificant. Finding the right situation means that the associate must seek others of like mind and beliefs who have made the same subjective choices.

People of like mind may be found among those who have attended the same school or have been in the same denomination for years. Graduates of the same school or members of the same denomination may not agree on every fine point, but the chances are higher that they will.

People of totally different backgrounds can still find doctrinal unanimity on a church staff. It will take time and effort to sort out the basics during the candidating process. As time goes by, the associate will have to determine if the newly discovered doctrinal differences are really heresy or simply differences of opinion. When it is determined that heresy has been found, then the associate has the option of raising the issue with the concerned staff member. If that does not solve the problem, one or two others should go to the concerned staff member and seek resolution. If there is none, the official board will become involved as representatives of the church.

It is conceivable that the staff member, the senior pastor, or the associate may be asked to resign. A church split may occur because of doctrinal heresy, so it is essential that the associate be certain of the issue selected for this kind of conflict. It may seem less complicated for the associate to resign than to drag the church through the pain that will be necessary to resolve the doctrinal issue.

One church staff had arguments over accepting members of the Masonic Lodge into membership. One staff member thought the Lodge believed in another gospel, whereas another did not. This issue was doctrinal in nature and if such members were allowed to join the church, this would seem to qualify as sufficient cause to clarify the doctrinal position of the church. If such clarification were not achieved, it seems to be sufficient cause for the associate's resignation.

Reason to Leave: Voted Out

This may seem obvious, but if the associate is ousted out by an official vote of the congregation, the associate may not need to resign. Resignation may precede such a meeting where it seems certain that the vote will be overwhelming. This scenario would occur only at the end of much negotiation and many other events. The vote of the congregation would only be necessary if the associate was adamant about his or her position and would not back down.

The associate may let the congregation vote without any influence from the associate or may form a coalition to support a particular point of view. It is reasoned that if the other side can form a coalition, then why can't the associate do the same? This line of thinking is a meaningless exercise. The motive might ostensibly be to get at the truth but could also be a way to punish the church for letting the associate go. The church business meeting will explode into accusations and counteraccusations among those in the coalitions. This scene can hardly be rationalized into being an event that brings glory to God. The only outcome that can be expected is bitterness, hostility, and disillusionment.

Another type of vote regarding pastoral staff is called a vote of confidence or a vote of no confidence. The vote may occur regularly at the annual church business meeting or it may take place at a specially called meeting. If the vote is taken regularly at the annual meeting, the occasion may be perfunctory and the result known in advance. If the meeting for such a vote is specially called, the occasion will not be merely perfunctory and the results will not be known in advance. If any change in the subject or subjects of the vote occurs—for example, the focus of the vote is switched from the senior pastor to a specific associate—the vote becomes special. As such, the vote takes on much more import.

When a vote of confidence is specially called for, there is a reason. This type of vote hopefully will be avoided by resolving the reason in advance. A vote of confidence involving the associate pastor is only one step away from the associate being asked to resign. If the vote is negative, or the vote is expected to be negative, the associate may have no choice but to resign. A vote of the church set for a future date may be adequate cause for an associate to seriously consider resignation.

Reason to Leave: Lack of Support

One reason to say yes to resignation could be the lack of support for the associate's ministry. This lack of support is not the occasional discouragements that come into the associate's life. This kind of no support is a direct statement from the senior pastor or from the official church board, or both, that the associate's ministry cannot continue and the associate's services are no longer wanted. What would cause them to say this to the associate?

The reasons for the senior pastor or official board to say the associate needed to move on are multiple. It would probably be impossible to list them all here, let alone discuss them in depth. There may be some cause to think of the associate as incompetent or in some way ill suited to the task assigned to him or her. There may be a kind of unresolvable conflict between an associate and someone else in the church. There may be some moral problem that has caused the associate to be deemed unfit for service in the church. Whatever the reason, when the associate hears that the services he or she rendered are no longer needed, the associate has sufficient reason to resign.

175

It is too bad if the situation deteriorates to the point where the associate no longer enjoys the support of the senior pastor or the board. Hopefully the problems that led up to this point would have been resolved before the associate is informed there is no more hope. The value of open and transparent communication is never more vividly demonstrated than in this situation.

For the associate, it comes down to the question, Do I really want to stay here? If the answer is yes, then the associate will institute a different plan of action than if the answer is no. In order to stay, it may be necessary for the associate to reevaluate his or her position. It may be necessary to change a position that has been held onto tenaciously. Humbling oneself before the church may be difficult, so it is important for the associate to choose his or her battles wisely.[1] One must make sure the issue is worth it and must try not to find oneself going through this procedure repeatedly. I would say lack of support is sufficient cause for an associate to resign.

Reason to Leave: Hypocrisy or Deceit

Another reason for resignation is the existence of hypocrisy or deceit on the part of those who supervise you. This is not poor communication based on a simple misunderstanding but the repeated stating of something that is contradicted by words or actions. If a person does not keep his or her word, then the foundation of the relationship is too fragile to build into an intimate friendship. The person who deceives or is a hypocrite has doubtful integrity. How much hypocrisy is acceptable in a working relationship on a church staff?

You may say that absolutely no hypocrisy of any kind should be accepted by a minister. This, of course, is an ideal that not many reach. If, for example, a senior pastor leads an associate to believe something that is not true about the pastor, is that hypocrisy or deceit? Are the sources for a sermon or Bible lesson given the credit for the ideas taken from them? Are program ideas completely original or borrowed from somewhere else? To say that everyone else takes from others without credit does not make it right. This is, of course, an ethical issue. Immorality takes many forms.

I am not saying that every mistake made by others who supervise the associate is cause for resignation. Mistakes can be and should be forgiven. I am saying that if the miscue is confronted directly, and the supervisor denies it, there is deceit. If it is done repeatedly, there is a pattern of hypocrisy. Hypocrisy like this eats away at a person's integrity and leads to mistrust and suspicion. I believe deceit and hypocrisy on the part of the associate's supervisors is adequate reason to resign.

Reason to Leave: Spouse Unsupportive

An unsupportive spouse is detrimental to the continuance of the associate's ministry. A spouse who occasionally complains about being left alone evenings or who feels unnecessary pressure from the associate's responsibilities in the church is not unsupportive. What I mean by an unsupportive spouse is one who questions the basic assumption that the associate should be in ministry at all.

Some associates may have entered the ministry before becoming married, and the spouse married into the ministry. The spouse may not have known what he or she was getting into. Other couples may have been married first and then the spouse had misgivings from the beginning, from when the associate declared interest in being in the ministry. The spouses's doubts about suitability or adequate skills of the associate may have been confirmed over the years. Each struggle or challenge becomes another example of the lack of the necessary competence. If the spouse continually affirms that the ministry should never have been entered, then the associate should seriously consider resigning.

A spouse who believes in the associate and in the value of the ministry is essential for those associates who are married. The ministry is difficult enough without a spouse's taking every opportunity to criticize or complain. Attacking the associate's personal worth as a minister will destroy the ministry as well as put the marriage in serious jeopardy. Any associate who has a spouse who does not want him or her in the ministry would have sufficient reason to resign.

Finishing Well

Once it is determined that an associate should resign, going through the process takes a bit of planning. The period from the time of the resignation to the actual farewell can be a very difficult period. One church I served required a two-month notice before leaving, but most require one month. Some resignations are immediately effective, but an official farewell is helpful for the church as well as the associate. It helps to provide a wrap-up for the years of service and to allay any suspicions about the situation surrounding the associate's departure.

Writing the resignation letter is important because the letter can be helpful or hurtful. If the letter criticizes the church or the leaders or rehearses the reasons why the resignation was so unfair, it becomes hurtful. If the letter refuses to get into the details of the resignation, it can be helpful. Those in the church who know, don't need to hear it again. Those who have no information about the details do not need to know or become a part of the problem. A simple letter that states the associate is resigning effective on a certain date and offers thanks is sufficient. Don't burn your bridges; you may want to go back to that church some day.

The timing of the resignation can be determined in consultation with the leaders of the church. There may be other activities to be held in the church that would conflict with a farewell, so dates must be carefully planned. It may be necessary to postpone the resignation until a better time for the farewell. It would be a mistake on the part of the associate to reject a farewell because the church and the associate needs closure.

I personally don't believe in resigning with no other position in the offering. This is often called "waiting on the Lord," but is a euphemism for resigning to nothing. Under certain circumstances, it may be necessary for the associate to resign thus. If, for example, the associate is forced out of ministry, it may be necessary to leave immediately. Finding another position may not be possible because of the lack of time. When an associate knows in advance of his or her eventual departure but resigns to nothing, it could appear that the church is forcing the associate out without allowing him or her to find another place.

I have already mentioned the futility of bargaining. If the associate has determined that resignation is inevitable, offering conditions of change in an attempt to rescind the resignation is useless and unwarranted.

It may be necessary to inform certain people in the church of your resignation so they are not offended by being told by someone else. These may be close friends or associates in the ministry who may be able to help with the transition to your next ministry.

Conclusion

It is important for an associate to finish well, at least as important as it is to begin and continue well. Knowing when it is right to resign will be helpful so that beautiful music may continue to pour forth from the associate's life.

Discussion Questions

Use these questions privately or in a group, such as a church staff, to apply the points made in this chapter.

1. How often have you thought about resignation in the last six months? Why?

2. Would you say you have experienced signs that you are under pressure to resign? What are they?

3. What have been the tenures of your service as an associate pastor? Have they been short or long? How would long tenure have helped your ministry to be more effective?

4. Have you been criticized by way of having you or your ministry compared to another? What have you done about it? What should you do about it?

5. How do you handle interpersonal conflict when it arises? Can you think of an example in your life and ministry?

6. Have you ever thought that you and your pastor have a difference in ministry philosophy? If so, about what specifically did you differ?

7. Have you ever made disparaging remarks about your senior pastor behind his back? What is the reason you use? What is the result of such behavior?

8. Does your church carry a long-term disability policy on you? Do you personally have such a policy? If not, why not?

9. Have promises that were made to you by your senior pastor or official board ever been broken or unfulfilled? What has been your reaction?

10. Are there differences in doctrine in your church that are sufficient cause for you to resign?

11. If a vote is called for at a special church business meeting regarding your continuance in your staff position at the church, would you resign before that time? Or would you dig in and fight? Explain your answer.

12. How do you feel about coalitions used for the purpose of supporting your position against the senior pastor or against the official church board?

13. What are some indications of lack of support for your ministry

that you might recognize from your senior pastor or official church board?

14. Are there examples of deceit or hypocrisy you have observed by those that supervise you? If yes, what will you do about it?

15. If you are married, would you say your spouse is supportive of your ministry? What makes you answer as you did?

16. How do you feel about resigning to nothing?

Guidelines for Choosing the Associate Pastorate

This appendix summarizes the salient points that should be considered before choosing to serve as an associate pastor. The questions will help the candidate evaluate the suitability of a church position in terms of his or her spiritual gifts, ministry skills, and talents.

Theological Agreement

1. Do you agree with the church's printed statement of faith in all respects?

2. Are there areas of disagreement that have been discovered? What will be done about the disagreements?

3. Do you expect to serve as an elder in this church? What is the church's expectation about the associate being spiritually qualified to be an elder? Does the church expect the associate to serve on the elder (or equivalent) board?

Church Traditions

1. With what church polity have you had the most ministry experience? What church polities can you work in without serious conflict?

2. Have you determined if the church operates as if there can be only one "holy man"? Can you function in your position as an associate if there is only one? Can you function as an associate if you are included as one of the "holy men"?

3. Have there been many others who have filled the associate position before in this church? How many have there been, and how long has each one stayed? Why did the last one leave?

4. What is the church's opinion about women serving as associate pastors? Do you agree?

5. Is the senior pastor's position regarding women as associates the same as yours?

The Minister

1. If asked by a search committee to share something from a recent personal Bible study and prayer time that has been meaningful to you, what would you share?

2. What are your specific spiritual gifts and how would they be employed in the associate position at the church?

3. Do you possess the spiritual gift(s) needed for this particular ministry in the church?

4. Are you willing to share elements of your personal life, such as integrity, self-esteem, vulnerability, and so on, with members of the search committee or the whole church? Will you do so if you are asked? What will you do if you are not asked about these things?

Church Expectations

1. Do you have a good understanding of what the church expects of its members (for example, amount of service)? How will church expectations of its members affect the tasks assigned to the associate?

2. Is the description of duties for the associate position presented in great detail, or is it general and vague? Which type of job description do you prefer? How will the description of duties be used to assess your ministry performance?

3. Are the church's expectations for the associate pastor realistic? Are they all written down? How might you find out?

4. Is the title being used for the new associate pastor understood by a wide spectrum of church members?

5. Does the church's description of duties for the associate position call for the associate to be more of a generalist or a specialist? Which do you prefer?

6. What provisions have been made for your development as an associate, either professionally or personally?

Expectations of the Associate

1. What do you perceive to be the expectations for the associate position from the church, the senior pastor, and the congregation? Can you live with those expectations?

2. What would make you believe that the relationship between you and the senior pastor will be what you expect it to be? What would not?

3. Have you thoroughly discussed the terms of salary and benefits? Have they been found satisfactory?

4. Have you asked the church how long the tenure of service for the associate pastor is expected to be? Does that time period match your expectation?

Relationship with Other Pastoral Staff Members

1. With whom do you expect to have close fellowship within the church staff or outside of it?

2. What would make you believe that the pastoral staff does not compete with each other or would not compete with you?

3. Have you explored the issue of conflict resolution with this

particular church staff? Are there examples you can give that illustrate good process?

Relationship with Church Members

1. Is there any evidence that indicates any resentment from church members about your coming as a new associate staff member? If so, why do they feel this way and what can be done about it?

2. Do you believe that people in the prospective church really believe as shown by their actions that every Christian is a worker, a staff member, in the body of Christ? How did you arrive at your conviction?

3. Does the prospective church operate more like an organization or more like an organism? How do you respond to that information? Will the answer affect your ministry as an associate?

4. Have you discovered what type of leader influence works best in the prospective church to get workers to enlist and continue to serve happily? Can you exercise that type of leader influence?

5. Do you know what the church practice is regarding the placement of people in service depending on their talents and spiritual gift(s)? Does the church require membership for service?

Relationship with Boards and Committees

1. Do you know what kind of role the associate is expected to play with the official board (servant, leader, antagonist, or equal)? Will you as an associate be expected to play a different role for a subcommittee of the official board?

2. Do you completely agree with the role that the official board expects the associate to fill?

3. Is there any conflict of interest regarding the supervision of you as an associate?

4. Are you aware of the makeup of the board or committee with which the associate will work (long- or short-term on committee, long- or short-time in church, planner or practitioner, etc.)? Is this acceptable to you?

Relationship with Outside Fellowships

1. Is the prospective church related to a denomination? If not, are you aware of any cooperation between the prospective church and other churches in the area?

2. What connections exist among the church and outside church fellowships? Are you comfortable with such connections?

3. Has this church participated with other churches in church-to-church activities? Will you be expected to participate in the future?

4. Do you know of other groups that the pastoral staff members meet with for fellowship? Who might those groups or individuals be?

Organizing for Success

1. Does the pastor of the church serve as the visionary for the church? How do you know? If not, who does serve as visionary? Does the church have a vision?

2. Will you as an associate be expected to manage a specific age group or the activities assigned to them? Is that acceptable to you?

3. Are you familiar with the five functions of management? Which one is easiest for you and which is the hardest? Which will be needed to fulfill the duties as described in the ministry description?

4. What is your style of leadership in most situations? Is that the style this particular church appreciates and needs at this time?

Modeling Faith to Family

1. If you have children and the search committee asks, will you permit the children to be interviewed? If you will not allow it, or it is not possible, how can you explain what your children think of the quality of your personal faith?

2. Are you prepared to share how your personal faith is modeled before your children?

3. Can you briefly describe what you expect from your children? Do you really expect perfection from them? What do you do when that is not what you receive?

4. Be prepared to describe the faith of each of your children and/or your spouse.

5. What condition exhibited by your children would cause you to resign as the associate in the church?

6. Your spouse should be prepared to reveal the level of support that exists for your ministry and how he or she plans to serve in the new church.

Termination

1. Be prepared to describe the conditions surrounding your resignation from your last place of ministry (your information might be compared to the facts gathered from other sources about your departure).

2. Be prepared to explore what might be legitimate reasons to cause you to resign from the church position.

3. Conversely, be prepared to explain the things that would not cause you to resign.

Other Issues

Feel free to construct other questions that you think will help you discover all you can about the position as associate in the church. It is far better to take the time to inquire thoroughly about the church than it is to rush into a relationship that turns sour because you did not do your homework. Doing a good job at the beginning will help you ensure that beautiful music will reverberate from the church staff you serve on for many years to come.

A Checklist for the Associate Pastor When Considering a Change

The issue of resignation will certainly be involved in making a change, but these questions will focus on different issues than those in chapter 13. These questions are designed to help an associate pastor determine if a change in the current place of ministry is warranted, or perhaps if a new place of service should be pursued. Accordingly, the questions will be organized around various categories.

Family

1. Is my family suffering because of my commitment to ministry involvement?

2. Am I able to give as much time and energy to my family as they need?

3. Are there major and continual complaints from my family about my being around too seldom?

4. Does my family support my ministry or do they seem to be fighting what I am trying to do in ministry?

5. Would a change in my ministry at this church affect my family in any way? What effect would there be on my family if I resigned and left this church?

6. Is the financial situation adequate for the needs of my family?

7. How has this current ministry been affecting my health and the health of my immediate family?

Ministry Impact

1. What impact is my ministry having in people's lives now compared to when I first began here? How do I know if there is an increase or decrease in impact?

2. Do I see more people excited about getting involved in my area of ministry because of my contribution to their lives, or are there fewer people?

3. Are there more people being reached now through the ministry I am responsible for than when I first began?

4. Are my spiritual gifts being utilized in the best possible way through my current ministry, or is there some way that a change in ministry focus would correct that?

5. Am I aware of how my spiritual gifts have been affirmed by those I have served in my current ministry? If yes, give examples. If no, why have my spiritual gifts not been confirmed?

6. Do my natural talents lend themselves to application in the role of the associate pastor? Am I doing what I generally like to do and am gifted to do? Is my ministry basically enjoyable, or do I dread it?

Unfinished Business

1. Has my ministry run its course, or is there more that needs to be done?

2. Do I have a long-term ministry plan that would be abbreviated if I left now?

3. What effect would my departure have on individuals in each area of my ministry?

4. If the vision of my church is clearly stated, is it one with which I can still agree and feel excited about? Or do I feel the church's vision is impossible to achieve (unrealistic), out of

date (stale), or missing the point entirely (wrong)? What can be done about it?

Potential

1. Is the potential I once saw in this place of ministry still there, or has something altered what I thought could be done?

2. Am I allowing an obstacle to block what God wants to do in this ministry in and through me? What might that obstacle be? What can be done to remove it?

3. Is someone else better suited to do what I have been attempting to do in my ministry?

4. Should I consider shifting to another aspect of ministry, either here or at another place? What might the reason(s) be?

Communication

1. Are the channels of communication open between me and others on the staff, especially between me and the senior pastor? What evidence can I cite to answer yes or no?

2. Is something "eating me up" and am I hiding it from those I minister with? Is that why I feel so uneasy about staying in my present ministry?

3. Do I feel that decisions are made in my area of responsibility without my input? If my input is requested for a decision in my area, is it followed? If it is not followed, are the reasons for taking another route reasonable or arbitrary? Do I feel I have been given the "run around"?

4. What evidences of support or lack of support for my ministry can I cite? What kind of support do I need but am not receiving?

5. Is my current dissatisfaction with my ministry worth "going to the wall" over, or can I find it within myself to overlook it?

Decision to Leave

1. Have I prayed about this decision to leave or am I letting my emotions dictate what I want to do?

2. Am I letting difficult circumstances turn my head toward "greener pastures"?

3. What from God's word has provided guidance for my decision? Am I interpreting the passage correctly or making it say what I want to read or to hear?

A Typical Candidating Sequence

The following steps are typical stages in the sequence of events that relate to the calling of an associate pastor by a local church. Not every church will follow these stages exactly, but they may serve as a guide for planning the process. A candidate may use these stages to learn, in general, what to expect from the candidating procedure. Each step should be prayerfully considered, and everyone involved should seek the will of God throughout every step in the candidating.

Determining Options

The first step is to discover what possibilities exist for the type of associate ministry desired. The possible sources of information will include placement offices in Christian colleges and/or seminaries, national or regional denominational offices, and placement services provided by national associate groups. One example of the latter is PACE, or Professional Association of Christian Educators. Other similar groups will likely have placement services also. Youth Specialties has a listing of openings on the Internet. The best source for discovering information about openings is the associate's personal network. Friends who know of current or potential situations will be the quickest source for information about where there is an opening. The network contacts can also become a good source of reference, since they know both the candidate and the situation that is opening.

Initial Contact

After prayerful consideration of the options, an initial contact is made with the church, usually by the candidate. If there is a referral involved, the initial contact can be made by the third party. The contact may be a phone call or letter to see if there still is an opening for a specific position. If the answer is affirmative, then the candidate's résumé is sent.

The résumé should be short; one page if possible. Every résumé should be written for the specific position open in that church. Include only information that has relevance to the specific position, such as how to make contact, family facts, ministry experience, education, training experiences, and so forth.

Information Requested

The search committee will sift through the various résumés and select those that seem to fit the profile of the person they need. Those possible candidates will be sent a request to provide more information. Those who do not fit the profile will usually be placed in an inactive file. Those in an inactive file may, or may not, be informed that they are not being pursued. Depending on how many résumés are received, information may be sought from a few to as many as twenty.

The form used to gather additional information may be designed by the search committee or obtained through another source. The regional or national offices of denominations have such forms and are willing to make them available to churches. Some ask detailed information about the candidate, such as the amount of debt the candidate carries. Names of references should be included. Sometimes a video or audio tape can be made by a candidate to provide the necessary information.

Initial Screening

The candidate is evaluated by each member of the search committee, who uses some form of assessing the candidate for each category. Sometimes the categories of the search committee don't match all the data requested by the information form. To make the screening process simpler, the evaluation form used by the search committee should try to follow the categories of the information form.

If a numbering system is used for each category, it is easy to determine which candidate has the highest total score. When each member is polled, the candidate with the highest score becomes the top candidate. Usually the candidates with the three highest total scores move on to the next stage.

References Checked

Contacting the references of the three chosen by the committee is the next step. References given by the candidate will likely be all positive, so the committee may see secondary references. Names suggested by the references will provide another dimension to the information needed on the candidate. Comparisons can also be made between the primary and secondary references.

The person or persons who supervised the candidate in the previous position should definitely be contacted. If the candidate is currently in a church, the committee should seek permission to talk with the senior pastor, even if his name is not given as a reference. All references gathered should have the difficult questions asked, so that as much information can be gathered as possible. You might want to use the questions in Appendix A of this book as a guide to some of the questions for the reference.

Preliminary Conference

The next stage is for the search committee to meet with the top three candidates. If the candidate lives close by, a personal visit can be arranged. If the candidate lives too far away for a visit, a conference telephone call should be arranged. Spouses (if the candidates have them) could also be invited to attend this get-acquainted meeting.

These conferences should be separate for each candidate, and it is best that they not include a Sunday service at the church. The session might be held at a home or at the church facility but not over a Sunday. This interview is not a candidating weekend—it is only to become better acquainted with the candidates.

Additional Information

There may have been some issues raised in the preliminary personal conference that require a bit more information. The search committee can request the additional details at this time. It does no good for the candidate to send any and all information to the committee before they ask for it. Candidates should wait until it becomes clear that they are one of the few (three?) being considered for the position.

Search committee members might visit the candidate to see the situation in which they are now serving. Some even ask members of the current church about the candidate. Even when this is done surreptitiously, most church members recognize a search committee when they arrive at a church and start asking questions. Individual inquiries can be made much more discreetly but do not generally result in as much information.

Candidate Selected

After the three candidates are interviewed as thoroughly as possible and all the necessary information has been found, the search committee prayerfully determines which of the three candidates will be the one presented to the church. If the committee is unanimous, the recommendation to the church is stronger.

The search committee chooses a candidate for the position and makes arrangements for that candidate and the spouse (and family if possible) to visit the church for a candidating weekend. Only one candidate should be presented to the church to avoid pitting one against the other or making the church choose among the three.

Candidating Interview

Assuming there is no reason to eliminate anyone, the top candidate for the position is invited to an extended interview by the search committee. The candidate is invited to take part in a series of events at the church. Various constituencies are invited to meet with the candidate at separate meetings. One of these groups must be the official board of the church.

Depending on what the associate's duties will be, the candidate is invited to participate in leading various groups during the visit. For example, if the position is minister of music, then the candidate will likely be asked to participate in some way in the music program during the visit. Unfortunately, these visits are usually very hectic and rushed, but they need not be. It is great if the period of candidating can be for a month or so, but most are limited to one weekend or even less.

It is my opinion that any candidate who agrees to come for a candidating weekend should be willing to go to the church if called. The candidate should be able to determine if there is a positive leading of the Lord to allow his or her name to stand as a candidate. If the candidate is unwilling to take the position if it is offered, then he or she should not go to the church for the candidating weekend. If the candidate is not sure, then more information must be sought from the church in order to make a decision. The church should not be required to cover the expenses of such a weekend if the candidate has no intention of accepting the call of the church.

If there are other churches being considered by the candidate, the church offering the candidating weekend should be informed. It is very likely that the candidate will be in communication with several churches, but if the conversation concerns a candidate visit, the candidate needs to decide which church he or she is considering first.

Church Decision

After the candidate has completed the candidating visit or visits to the church, the church decides on the recommendation of the search committee. If the church polity is congregational, a special business meeting is announced for the purpose of considering the candidate.

Sometimes the vote is held the Sunday night of the candidating weekend, but it should be delayed if at all possible. This gives the church time to pray about the decision. It also allows time to gather more information, should it be desired. If the church is elder run, the call is decided on by the elder board and announced to the church.

Not many all-church votes of this type will be 100 percent to affirm, especially on the first ballot. Some churches require a certain percentage of their members to be present at a meeting to call a pastoral-staff member. Others might require a certain percentage of the vote in order to call any specific candidate. The decision of the church is communicated to the candidate along with the terms of the call, including salary and benefits. A phone call provides the immediate information and should be followed up by a formal letter that details the same information.

Candidate Responds

After the church has explained all aspects of the call to the candidate, the candidate responds to the church in some formal way. A phone call will tell the senior pastor or the search committee chairman what the decision is, but a formal letter will confirm it. Details to be confirmed should include the salary, benefits, start date for the new ministry, and moving expenses covered if any.

The response of the candidate should be positive since the decision was to go to the church if they called. It is possible that some unforeseen event or situation has arisen that might change that decision, but generally the response should be yes if the candidate has proceeded this far with the church.

Move to New Ministry

The candidate announces the resignation to the current church and participates in the farewell. Arrangements are made for moving to the new location and ministry.

Bibliography

Arndt, F. W., and F. W. Gingrich. *A Greek-English Lexicon of the New Testament and Other Early Christian Literature*. 4th ed. Revised and Augmented. Chicago: University of Chicago Press, 1957.

Augsberger, D. *Caring Enough to Confront*. Ventura, Calif.: Regal Books, 1981.

Bandura, A. *Social Foundations of Thought and Action: A Social Cognitive Theory*. Englewood Cliffs, N.J.: Prentice-Hall Publishers, 1986.

Bass, B. M. *Stodgill's Handbook of Leadership*. New York: Free Press, 1981.

Bufford, R. *The Human Reflex: Behavioral Psychology in Biblical Perspective*. San Francisco: Harper & Row, 1981.

Bushnell, H. *Christian Nurture*. Grand Rapids: Baker, 1979.

Campolo, T. *The Power Delusion*. Wheaton, Ill.: Victor Books, 1983.

Charles E. Fuller Institute, P.O. Box 91990, Pasadena, CA 91109-1990. Phone 1-800-999-9578.

Christian Impact Ministries, "The Combination Personality and Spiritual Gifts Inventory." Uniquely You Resources, P. O. Box 490, Blue Ridge, GA 30513. Phone 1-800-501-0490 or 706-632-8411.

Church and Community Survey Workbook: A Guide for Identifying Church Needs. Nashville: Broadman, 1970.

Council on Biblical Manhood and Womanhood, P.O. Box 7337, Libertyville, Ill. 60048.

Edwards, G. *A Tale of Three Kings: A Study in Brokenness*. Augusta, Maine: Christian Books, 1980.

Erikson, E. *Childhood and Society*. 2d ed. New York: W. W. Norton & Co., 1950, 1963.

———. *Identity: Youth and Crisis*. New York: W. W. Norton & Co., 1968.

Ford, L. *Design for Teaching and Training*. Nashville, Tenn.: Broadman, 1978.

Gardner, J. *The Nature of Leadership*. Washington, D.C.: Independent Sector, 1986.

Getz, G. *The Measure of a Man*. Glendale, Calif.: Regal Books, 1974.

———. *Sharpening the Focus of the Church*. Chicago: Moody, 1974.

Habecker, E. B. "Power, Authority & Christian Organizational Leadership: A Call for Followership." *Crux*, vol. 26, no. 4 (December 1990).

House, H. W., ed. *Divorce and Remarriage: Four Christian Views*. Downers Grove, Ill.: InterVarsity, 1990.

Jones, Jerry, ed. "What You Need to Know to More Effectively Recruit Volunteers." *SAM Journal*, no. 122 (May/June 1997): 1.

Kast, F. E., and J. E. Rosenzweig. *Organization and Management*. New York: McGraw-Hill, 1974.

Kostenberger, A. J., T. R. Schreiner, and H. S. Baldwin, eds. "An Interpretation of 1 Timothy 2:9–15: A Dialog with Scholarship." In *Women in the Church*. Grand Rapids: Baker, 1995.

Langham, I. *The Building of British Social Anthropology*. Boston: D. Reidel, 1981.

Lawson, K. E. "The Current State of the Educational Ministry Profession Part One." *Christian Education Journal* 16, no. 1 (fall 1995): 9–27.

———. "Former Directors of Christian Education—Why They Left: Implications for the Profession." *Christian Education Journal* 14, no. 2 (winter 1994): 46–63.

———. "Summary Report: Current and Former Educational Ministry Staff in North America." An unpublished manuscript, May 1994.

Lawson, M. S., and R. J. Choun Jr. *Directing Christian Education: The Changing Role of the Christian Education Specialist*. Chicago: Moody, 1992.

Lightfoot, J. P. *Saint Paul: The Epistle to the Philippians*. London: MacMillan, 1881.

Mackenzie, R. A. "The Management Process in 3–D." *Harvard Business Review*, November–December 1969.

Orr, J., ed. *The International Standard Bible Encyclopaedia*. Vol. 2. Grand Rapids: Eerdmans, 1960.

Schaller, L. *Multiple Staff in the Larger Church*. Nashville: Abingdon, 1980.

Smith, David. *The Friendless American Male*. Ventura, Calif.: Regal Books, 1983.

Smith, Donald. *Creating Understanding*. Grand Rapids: Zondervan, 1992.

Tenney, M. C. *The Zondervan Pictorial Bible Dictionary*. Grand Rapids: Zondervan, 1963.

The Analytical Greek Lexicon. Grand Rapids: Zondervan, 1970–73.

Walvoord, J., and R. Zuck, eds. *The Bible Knowledge Commentary, Old Testament*. Wheaton, Ill.: Victor, 1985.

Warren, R. *The Purpose Driven Church*. Grand Rapids: Zondervan, 1995.

White, B. *The First Three Years of Life*. Englewood Cliffs, N.J.: Prentice-Hall, 1975.

Wiebe, Ronald W., and Bruce A. Rowlinson. *Let's Talk About Church Staff Relationships*. Alhambra, Calif.: Green Leaf Press, 1983.

Willowcreek Community Church, South Barrington, Ill. (www.willowcreek.org).

Woodruff, M. "Criticism: The Breakfast of Champions." In *Youthworker Journal*, vol. 12, no. 4 (May/June 1996).

Wuest, K. *Word Studies in the Greek New Testament*. Vol. 1. *Ephesians and Colossians in the Greek New Testament*. Grand Rapids: Eerdmans, 1966.

Zondervan Church Source, P.O. Box 668, Holmes, PA 19043-9631. Phone 1-800-727-3480.

Notes

Preface

1. K. E. Lawson, "Summary Report: Current and Former Church Educational Ministry Staff in North America," 1994, 5. Available from the author at Talbot School of Theology, 13800 Biola Ave., La Mirada, CA 90639.

Chapter One

1. Following the guidelines of Lyle Schaller, a large church has between 225 and 450 members. See L. Schaller, *Multiple Staff in the Larger Church* (Nashville: Abingdon, 1980), 31.
2. J. Orr, ed., *The International Standard Bible Encyclopaedia*, vol. 2 (Grand Rapids: Eerdmans, 1960), 924.
3. M. C. Tenney, *The Zondervan Pictorial Bible Dictionary* (Grand Rapids: Zondervan, 1963), 241.
4. *The Analytical Greek Lexicon to the New Testament* (Grand Rapids: Zondervan, 1970–1973), 381.
5. F. W. Arndt and F. W. Gingrich, *A Greek-English Lexicon of the New Testament and Other Early Christian Literature*, 4th ed. (Chicago, Ill.: Univ. of Chicago Press, 1957).
6. Ibid., 783.
7. J. P. Lightfoot, *Saint Paul: The Epistle to the Philippians* (London: MacMillan, 1881), 95.
8. Arndt and Gingrich, *A Greek-English Lexicon*, 299.
9. Lightfoot, *Saint Paul*, 96.
10. Thinking of these two titles as one office is a result of applying the Granville Sharp rule. See Kenneth Wuest, *Word Studies in the Greek New Testament*, vol. 1, *Ephesians and Colossians in the Greek New Testament* (Grand Rapids: Eerdmans, 1966), 101.
11. G. Getz, *Sharpening the Focus of the Church* (Chicago: Moody, 1974), 110.
12. Ibid., 95.
13. Ibid., 96.
14. Ibid.
15. See Arndt and Gingrich, *A Greek-English Lexicon*, 99.
16. G. Getz, *The Measure of a Man* (Wheaton, Ill.: Victor, 1974), 27–35.

17. The issue of a woman's serving as an associate will be discussed in the next chapter.
18. There are various points of view about divorce. For an excellent summary of the various positions on this subject, see H. Wayne House, ed., *Divorce and Remarriage: Four Christian Views* (Wheaton, Ill.: InterVarsity, 1990).

Chapter Two

1. The polity of some Christian churches not usually thought of as Protestant evangelical (Roman Catholic or Eastern Orthodox) might be similar to the descriptions used in this chapter, but I have not intended to describe their polity in this description.
2. T. R. Schreiner, "An Interpretation of 1 Timothy 2:9–15: A Dialog with Scholarship," in *Women in the Church*, ed. A. J. Kostenberger, T. R. Schreiner, and H. S. Baldwin (Grand Rapids: Baker, 1995), 134.
3. Ibid., 105.
4. There are excellent materials on this subject available from the Council on Biblical Manhood and Womanhood, P.O. Box 7337, Libertyville, IL 60048.
5. Kostenberger, Schreiner, and Baldwin, *Women in the Church*, 211.

Chapter Three

1. David Smith, *The Friendless American Male* (Ventura, Calif.: Regal, 1983).
2. The "Combination Personality and Spiritual Gifts Inventory" is produced by Christian Impact Ministries, Uniquely You Resources, P.O. Box 490, Blue Ridge, GA 30513; 1-800-501-0490 or 706-632-8411.
3. Ibid., 4.
4. Other kinds of goals would be knowledge, understanding, and attitudes or values. See LeRoy Ford's book, *Design for Teaching and Training* (Nashville: Broadman, 1978) for more information about educational goals and chapter 5 of Donald Smith's book *Creating Understanding* (Grand Rapids: Zondervan, 1992).
5. Michael Woodruff, "Criticism: The Breakfast of Champions," *Youthworker Journal* 12, no. 4 (May/June 1996): 8–13.

Chapter Four

1. R. Warren, *The Purpose Driven Church* (Grand Rapids: Zondervan, 1995), 343.
2. M. S. Lawson and R. J. Choun, Jr., *Directing Christian Education:*

The Changing Role of the Christian Education Specialist (Chicago: Moody, 1992), 286.

3. K . E. Lawson, "The Current State of the Educational Ministry Profession Part One: Perspectives from the Front Lines," *Christian Education Journal* 16, no. 1 (fall 1995): 16.

4. This title is used at the Mountain View Christian Church, Gresham, Oregon.

Chapter Five

1. I. Langham, *The Building of British Social Anthropology* (Boston: Reidel, 1981), 245.

2. K. E. Lawson, "The Current State of the Educational Ministry Profession Part One," *Christian Education Journal* 16, no. 1 (fall 1995): 13.

Chapter Six

1. K. E. Lawson, "Former Directors of Christian Education— Why They Left: Implications for the Profession," *Christian Education Journal* 14, no. 2 (winter 1994): 57–58.

2. E. B. Habecker, "Power, Authority and Christian Organizational Leadership: A Call for Followership," *Crux* 26, no. 4 (December 1990): 11.

3. F. E. Kast and J. E. Rosenzweig, *Organization and Management* (New York: McGraw-Hill, 1974), 335.

4. J. Gardner, *The Nature of Leadership* (Washington, D.C.: Independent Sector, 1986), 7.

5. Habecker, "Power, Authority and Christian Organizational Leadership," 13.

6. An excellent treatment of power in the ministry is Tony Campolo's *The Power Delusion* (Wheaton, Ill.: Victor, 1983).

7. David Smith, *The Friendless American Male* (Ventura, Calif.: Regal, 1983).

Chapter Seven

1. An excellent guide for resolving conflicts is David Augsberger's book, *Caring Enough to Confront* (Ventura, Calif.: Regal, 1981).

Chapter Eight

1. Jerry Jones, ed., "What You Need to Know to More Effectively Recruit Volunteers," *SAM Journal*, no. 122 (May/June 1997): 1.

2. R. Bufford, *The Human Reflex: Behavioral Psychology in Biblical Perspective* (San Francisco: Harper and Row, 1981), 4.

3. Ibid., 5.
4. Ibid., 11.
5. Ibid., 12.
6. Ibid., 14.
7. Jones, "What You Need to Know to More Effectively Recruit Volunteers," 1.
8. The Uniquely You Combination Profile can be used, or separate spiritual gift inventories are available. Four different kinds of spiritual gift inventories based on theological position are available from the Charles E. Fuller Institute, P.O. Box 91990, Pasadena, CA 91109-1990; 1-800-999–9578.
9. For more information, contact Willow Creek Community Church at their web site, www.willowcreek.org or the Charles E. Fuller Institute, P.O. Box 91990, Pasadena, CA 91109-1990; 1-800-999-9578.
10. Available through Zondervan Church *Source*, P.O. Box 668, Holmes, PA 19043-9631; 1-800-727-3480.

Chapter Eleven

1. R. Alex Mackenzie, "The Management Process in 3–D," *Harvard Business Review* (November–December 1969), 80–87.
2. Detailed analyses are not required to discover valuable information. See *Church and Community Survey Workbook: A Guide for Identifying Church Needs* (Nashville: Broadman, 1970) for more information on evaluating your church.
3. See chapter 3 for more complete definitions of the terms *purpose*, *goal*, and *objectives*.
4. Motivation of unpaid staff is also discussed in chapter 8.
5. B. M. Bass, *Stodgill's Handbook of Leadership* (New York: Free Press, 1981), chapter 3.
6. P. Hersey and K. H. Blanchard, "Life Cycle Theory of Leadership," *Training and Development Journal* (1969), 23, 26–34.
7. Ibid., 34.
8. This event had or has no connection with the national youth ministry of the Annual Meeting of Friends (Quakers) that uses the same name.

Chapter Twelve

1. A. Bandura, *Social Foundations of Thought and Action: A Social Cognitive Theory* (Englewood Cliffs, N.J.: Prentice-Hall, 1986).
2. Ibid., 70.
3. A. Bandura and R. W. Jeffrey, "Role of Symbolic Coding and Rehearsal Processes in Observational Learning," *Journal of*

Personality and Social Psychology (1973), 26, 122–130. See also G. Comstock, S. Chaffee, N. Katzman, M. McCombs, and D. Roberts, *Television and Human Behavior* (New York: Columbia University Press, 1978); and R. M. Liebert, J. N. Sprafkin, and E. S. Davidson, *The Early Window: Effects of Television on Children and Youth*, 2d ed. (Elmsford, N.Y.: Pergamon, 1982).
4. Bandura, *Social Foundations of Thought and Action*, 71.
5. B. White, *The First Three Years of Life* (Englewood Cliffs, N.J.: Prentice-Hall, 1975), xi.
6. Bushnell said a child raised in a Christian home would grow up a Christian, never having known otherwise. His landmark book of 1861 has become the most popular position of the reformed theologians about childhood conversions. See H. Bushnell, *Christian Nurture* (Grand Rapids: Baker, 1979), 10.
7. J. Walvoord and R. Zuck, eds., *The Bible Knowledge Commentary, Old Testament* (Wheaton, Ill.: Victor, 1985), 953.
8. Some parents have reported that they began singing and reading to their unborn child and claimed the child's subsequent behavior had been influenced. It is known that an unborn child recognizes sounds while still in the womb. Whether or not the child's behavior after birth is affected by sounds heard in the womb is speculative and unknown.
9. This concept was originally expounded by Erik Erikson in *Childhood and Society*, 2d ed. (New York: W. W. Norton & Co., 1950, 1963) and *Identity: Youth and Crisis* (New York: W. W. Norton & Co., 1968). He describes the struggle of adolescence as identity vs. role confusion.

Chapter Thirteen
1. An excellent treatment of humility in ministry is Gene Edwards's book *A Tale of Three Kings: A Study in Brokenness* (Augusta, Maine: Christian Books, 1980).